TO:

FROM:

Praise the Lord, O my soul;
all my inmost being, praise his holy name.
Psalm 103:1

DAILY PRAISE

FROM THE NEW INTERNATIONAL VERSION

inspirio™

INTRODUCTION

We serve a great and mighty God—a God worthy of our continual praise and adoration. So majestic and unsearchable is he that he is represented by more than three hundred names within the text of Scripture. Many of these names describe aspects of his character—his kindness, his mercy, his love, his goodness, while others attempt to define the many roles he plays in our lives—counselor, teacher, savior, shepherd. These names have been given to identify for us the many reflections of a God so great that we can know him only as he reveals himself to us in the context of our need.

In the pages of this book, you will find a new reason each day to enthusiastically praise God for all that he is and all that he has done for you. Open your heart to a new level of worship as you feed day-by-day on the unfathomable majesty of his person.

O God, you are my God. . . .
Because your love is better than life,
my lips will glorify you.
I will praise you as long as I live,
and in your name I will lift up my hands.
Psalm 63:1, 3–4

*God exalted Christ to the highest place
and gave him the name that is above every name,
that at the name of Jesus every knee should bow,
in heaven and on earth and under the earth,
and every tongue confess that Jesus Christ is Lord,
to the glory of God the Father.*
PHILIPPIANS 2:9–11

We often go through the motions of worship with our heads, but never let our hearts into the process. We sit and sing the hymns during worship, but our hearts are concerned with paying the dentist bill or handling a problem with our in-laws.

To truly worship God we need our heads and our hearts. We must clear our minds of the mundane worries that plague us and respond to God by recognizing the wonders of his person and experiencing the truths he shows us about himself. Only then will he be able to worship God "in spirit and in truth" (John 4:24).

SARAH M. HUPP

GOD THE CREATOR

ELOHIM

*In the beginning God created
the heavens and the earth.*

GENESIS 1:1

You alone chose to create all things, to make a world to glorify Yourself and to receive Your love. You alone, in the mystery of Your sovereignty, chose me even before the creation of the world to belong to You as your special, beloved child. I am amazed, awestruck, humbled, beloved—and I bow before You alone.

NIV WORSHIP BIBLE

AS YOU PRAISE GOD TODAY

- Thank God for creating you and for the beauty of his creation around you.
- Consider how amazing it is that God made the earth and the universe out of nothing—with just a word.
- Pray this verse: "Creator God, by you all things were created: things in heaven and on earth, visible and invisible, whether thrones or powers or rulers or authorities; all things were created by you and for you" (Colossians 1:16).

SPIRIT OF GOD

Those who are led by the Spirit of God
are sons of God.
ROMANS 8:14

Who among men knows the thoughts of a man
except the man's spirit within him? In the same
way no one knows the thoughts of God except
the Spirit of God.
1 CORINTHIANS 2:11

The Spirit of God has the habit of taking the words of Jesus out of their scriptural setting and putting them into the setting of our personal lives.

OSWALD CHAMBERS

AS YOU PRAISE GOD TODAY

- Allow God to lead you by his Spirit and reveal his thoughts to you. Give him praise as you allow yourself to be filled with his presence.
- Thank God for enabling you to recognize the Spirit of God.

THE SELF-EXISTING ONE

JEHOVAH

"I am the Alpha and the Omega,"
says the Lord God, "who is, and who was,
and who is to come, the Almighty."
REVELATION 1:8

In the beginning you laid the foundations of
the earth, and the heavens are the work
of your hands. You remain the same,
and your years will never end.
PSALM 102:25, 27

AS YOU PRAISE GOD TODAY

- Call him Jehovah, the Self Existent One.
- Jehovah is a relational name of God. Thank him for keeping his covenant with you—for a relationship with him as LORD God.
- Write down three ways that God has kept and strengthened his relationship with you in the past year.

GOD IS MORE THAN ABLE

Ah, Sovereign LORD, you have made the heavens and the earth by your great power and out-stretched arm. Nothing is too hard for you.
JEREMIAH 32:17

"I am the LORD, the God of all mankind. Is anything too hard for me?"

JEREMIAH 32:27

AS YOU PRAISE GOD TODAY

- Give God praise, honor, and glory for being more than able to handle anything you bring to him in prayer.
- Praise him because *nothing* is too difficult for him.

TO BE STRONG

Moses and the Israelites sang this song to the LORD:
"The LORD is my strength and my song;
he has become my salvation."

EXODUS 15:2

I will sing of your strength,
in the morning I will sing of your love;
for you are my fortress,
my refuge in times of trouble.
O my Strength, I sing praise to you;
you, O God, are my fortress, my loving God.

PSALM 59:16–17

AS YOU PRAISE GOD TODAY

- Praise him for his strength, which he uses on your behalf.
- Thank God for his strong guidance in your life.
- Join with the Psalmist in singing praises for God's strength.

MOST HIGH

EL ELYON

You, O LORD, are the Most High
over all the earth;
you are exalted far above all gods.

PSALM 97:9

When I look at the majesty of the mountains, I cannot help but praise God. Those mountains are so mammoth, so strong, immovable. Higher than the highest mountain, even higher than the highest heavens, is where our God is enthroned. Not only is he Most High in his location, but he is also Most High in his authority—higher than any king or president, higher than any prime minister or ruler. In addition, he is Most High in his wisdom and Most High in his love. Truly he is Most High in *all* things.

AS YOU PRAISE GOD TODAY

- Think of three more ways that God is Most High in your life.
- Pray Psalm 97:9 above.

GOD IS BEYOND COMPREHENSION

God performs wonders that cannot be fathomed,
miracles that cannot be counted.

JOB 5:9

Do you not know?
Have you not heard?
The LORD is the everlasting God,
the Creator of the ends of the earth.
He will not grow tired or weary,
and his understanding no one can fathom.

ISAIAH 40:28

AS YOU PRAISE GOD TODAY

- Think of it—God is beyond anything you could possibly comprehend. Give him a shout of praise.
- Pray the prayer in Ephesians 1:17–20 and praise God for opening the eyes of your heart.

THE FATHER COMMANDED THE ANGELS TO WORSHIP HIS SON

*When God brings his firstborn into the world, he says,
"Let all God's angels worship him."*

HEBREWS 1:6

*The angel said to the shepherds, "Do not be
afraid. I bring you good news of great joy that
will be for all the people. Today in the town of
David a Savior has been born to you; he is Christ
the Lord. This will be a sign to you: You will find
a baby wrapped in cloths and lying in a manger."
Suddenly a great company of the heavenly host
appeared with the angel, praising God and saying,
"Glory to God in the highest,
and on earth peace to men on whom his favor rests."*

LUKE 2:10–14

AS YOU PRAISE GOD TODAY

- Join with the angels in praising God for sending
  Christ the Lord.
- Rejoice that what was good news of great joy the
  night of Jesus' birth is good news for you today!

THE LORD THAT SEES ALL THINGS

EL ROI

Hagar gave this name to the LORD who spoke to her: "You are the God who sees me," for she said, "I have now seen the One who sees me."

GENESIS 16:13

Our all-knowing, all-wise God is also our all-seeing God. His presence permeates everything we do. We live and move and have our being in him. We walk before him each day, our hearts opened before him. He sees our pain, our discouragement, our confusion, our heartache, our struggles. And in the seeing, he comes to our rescue with amazing grace.

CHARLES STANLEY

AS YOU PRAISE GOD TODAY

- Think about the fact that God sees your every thought and every action and still loves you!
- Thank him for always watching over your loved ones when they are away from you.
- Think back to a time when you were hurting. Praise God for seeing your tears and coming to your aid.

ANGEL OF THE LORD

*When Gideon realized that it was the angel of
the LORD, he exclaimed, "Ah, Sovereign LORD! I
have seen the angel of the LORD face to face!"
But the LORD said to him, "Peace! Do not be
afraid. You are not going to die."*

JUDGES 6:22–23

*The angel of the LORD encamps around
those who fear him,
and he delivers them.*

PSALM 34:7

AS YOU PRAISE GOD TODAY

- Think of Gideon's disbelief when the angel of
  the Lord appeared to him.
- Think of one way God has protected you from
  harm this past week.
- Praise him for the various ways he speaks to you
  and protects you.

GOD IS ALL-SUFFICIENT

EL SHADDAI

*He who dwells in the shelter of the Most High
will rest in the shadow of the Almighty.
I will say of the LORD, "He is my refuge
and my fortress,
my God, in whom I trust."*

PSALM 91:1–2

Have I placed my confidence in God Himself, not in His blessings? For God says: "I am Almighty God"—El Shaddai, the All-Powerful God (Genesis 17:1). Nothing that other saints do or say can upset the one who is built on God.

OSWALD CHAMBERS

AS YOU PRAISE GOD TODAY

- Thank him that he is the All-Sufficient One, someone you can lean on and find all you need all the time.
- Was there a time when you relied on yourself and not on God? How did the situation turn out?
- Praise God for giving you abilities you never would have had without him.

GOD IS A TRINITY

*May the grace of the Lord Jesus Christ,
and the love of God, and the fellowship
of the Holy Spirit be with you all.*
2 CORINTHIANS 13:14

*To God's elect ... who have been chosen
according to the foreknowledge of God the Father,
through the sanctifying work of the Spirit, for
obedience to Jesus Christ and
sprinkling by his blood:
Grace and peace be yours in abundance.*
1 PETER 1:1–2

AS YOU PRAISE GOD TODAY

• Ponder the wonder of God being three persons
  yet one: Father, Son, and Holy Spirit.

GOD IS THE GIVER OF RAINS

"I will send rain on your land in its season, both autumn and spring rains, so that you may gather in your grain, new wine and oil."
DEUTERONOMY 11:14

You care for the land and water it;
you enrich it abundantly.
The streams of God are filled with water
to provide the people with grain,
for so you have ordained it.
You drench its furrows
and level its ridges;
you soften it with showers
and bless its crops.
PSALM 65:9–10

AS YOU PRAISE GOD TODAY

- Praise God for being the giver of rains, abundant showers.
- Praise him for softening the ground with showers and blessing it with crops.
- Thank God for sending rain in the proper seasons.

THE LORD WILL PROVIDE

JEHOVAH JIREH

*Abraham built an altar and arranged the wood on it.
He bound his son Isaac and laid him on the altar. . . .
Then he reached out his hand and took the knife
to slay his son.
The angel of the LORD called out to him from heaven,
"Abraham! Abraham!" "Here I am," he replied.
"Do not lay a hand on the boy," he said. "Do not do
anything to him. Now I know that you fear God,
because you have not withheld from me your son,
your only son."
Abraham looked up and there in a thicket he saw a
ram caught by its horns. He . . . took the ram and
sacrificed it as a burnt offering instead of his son. So
Abraham called that place The LORD Will Provide.
And to this day it is said, "On the mountain of the
LORD it will be provided."*

GENESIS 22:9–14

AS YOU PRAISE GOD TODAY

- Call God Jehovah-Jireh, your faithful provider, and read these promises from his Word: Psalm 111:5, Isaiah 58:11, Acts 14:17, 1 Timothy 6:17.
- Thank God for supplying all your needs. Let go of your worries and anxieties, and instead see God as your source of all you need.

GOD BESTOWS PEACE

I will lie down and sleep in peace,
for you alone, O LORD,
make me dwell in safety.
PSALM 4:8

When winds are raging o'er the upper ocean,
And waves are tossed wild with an angry roar,
It's said, far down beneath the wild commotion,
That peaceful stillness reigns forevermore.

Far, far away, the roars of strife fall silent,
And loving thoughts rise ever peacefully,
And no storm, however fierce or violent,
Disturbs the soul that rests, O Lord in Thee.
HARRIET BEECHER STOWE

AS YOU PRAISE GOD TODAY

- Do not be afraid. Praise God for granting you his peace and peaceful sleep.
- Praise God for making a covenant of peace with you so that you will not be shaken, regardless of the circumstances in which you find yourself.

GOD IS YOUR SHEPHERD

JEHOVAH-ROHI

The LORD is my shepherd, I shall not be in want.
He makes me lie down in green pastures,
he leads me beside quiet waters,
he restores my soul.
He guides me in paths of righteousness
for his name's sake.

PSALM 23:1–3

"The Lord's My Shepherd." This beautiful, meta-phorical hymn embraces the complete needs of man. Nothing could be dearer in life or death!

LEROY BROWNLOW

AS YOU PRAISE GOD TODAY

- Thank him for loving you, taking care of you, and protecting you as a shepherd cares for his sheep.
- Read these verses about how God serves as your loving Shepherd: Isaiah 40:11; Ezekiel 34:12, 16; and Micah 5:4, 7:14.
- Now praise God that you can understand his shepherding voice when he speaks.

GOD IS THE MIGHTY ONE

ABHIR

The Mighty One, God, the LORD,
speaks and summons the earth
from the rising of the sun to the place where it sets.
PSALM 50:1

"You will know that I, the LORD, am your Savior,
your Redeemer, the Mighty One of Jacob."
ISAIAH 60:16

AS YOU PRAISE GOD TODAY

- Glorify God for his mighty works!
- Rejoice that he is the Mighty One in your life—performing his Word, guarding your life, and ruling the earth and universe.
- Praise God for his strength and power that are far above that of all people.
- Picture his strong arms lifting you up when you get into trouble.

JESUS IS THE CORNERSTONE

*You are no longer foreigners and aliens,
but fellow citizens with God's people and members of God's household, built on the foundation
of the apostles and prophets, with Christ Jesus
himself as the chief cornerstone.*

EPHESIANS 2:19–20

*As you come to him, the living Stone—rejected
by men but chosen by God and precious to
him—you also, like living stones, are being
built into a spiritual house to be a holy
priesthood, offering spiritual sacrifices acceptable
to God through Jesus Christ.*

1 PETER 2:4–5

Jesus is a Living Stone, the Cornerstone of his Church. I wonder what the final Church will look like. A cathedral? A little country chapel? A medieval master-piece? What a beautiful picture and a glorious reality!

AS YOU PRAISE GOD TODAY

- Meditate on the verses on this page, especially 1 Peter 2:4–5 and what they mean for you.
- Praise Jesus for the sure foundation he lays for us.

THE LORD IS
YOUR BANNER

JEHOVAH-NISSI

*Moses built an altar and called it
The LORD is my Banner.*
EXODUS 17:15

*We will shout for joy when you are victorious
and will lift up our banners in
the name of our God.*
PSALM 20:5

Jehovah-Nissi, our Banner, is a symbol of victory
in warfare. When you need a miracle, the Lord
your Banner is able to do it for you. He is your standard in the battle of everyday life. In the midst of
life's raging battles, you can see him high and lifted
up—if you keep our eyes on him and follow him,
you will be miraculously victorious.

AS YOU PRAISE GOD TODAY

- Praise him for being your Banner, symbolizing
victory in your life.
- Shout for joy and lift up a banner in celebration.

I AM

> *God said to Moses, "I AM WHO I AM.*
> *This is what you are to say to the Israelites:*
> *'I AM has sent me to you.'"*
> EXODUS 3:14

I tremble before Your presence, Lord. I am both humbled and hopeful at the revelation of Your name and the awesome power of Your being. You are the I AM, the eternal majestic One, Yahweh!

NIV WORSHIP BIBLE

AS YOU PRAISE GOD TODAY

- Read the following Scriptures and notice the ways Jesus says, "I AM": John 8:12; 9:5; 10:11,14; 11:25; 14:6; 15:1,5.
- What is one way that God has shown his trustworthiness to you in the past year?
- Give God your thanks and praise for being trustworthy.

THE GOD OF ABRAHAM, ISAAC, AND JACOB

*God ... said to Moses, "Say to the Israelites,
'The Lord, the God of your fathers—the God
of Abraham, the God of Isaac and the God
of Jacob—has sent me to you.' This is my name
forever, the name by which I am to be
remembered from generation to generation."*
EXODUS 3:15

*The God of Abraham, Isaac and Jacob, the God
of our fathers, has glorified his servant Jesus.*
ACTS 3:13

AS YOU PRAISE GOD TODAY

- Thank God for being your covenant-keeping God, the same God who kept his promises to Abraham, Isaac, and Jacob.
- Remember how he has kept his promises to you and your family in the past and give him praise.

FATHER

How great is the love the Father has lavished on us, that we should be called children of God! And that is what we are!

1 JOHN 3:1

"I will be a Father to you, and you will be my sons and daughters," says the Lord Almighty.

2 CORINTHIANS 6:18

As much as we love our sometimes unruly children, God loves us more. With the love of a parent who loves a child regardless—God loves us. We trip over our stupidity and fall, making a mess of what God has planned for us. The humor in the moment strikes him. How can he be angry? He loves us with the unchanging, lavish love of a Father.

AS YOU PRAISE GOD TODAY

- Rejoice that God is a perfect loving Father—his love and faithfulness far exceed that of even the best earthly dad.
- Look at a picture of your dad and think of one way that he reflected the love of God in your life. Give your heavenly Father thanks.

THE LORD WHO HEALS

JEHOVAH ROPHE

"I am the LORD, who heals you."
EXODUS 15:26

*The LORD heals the brokenhearted
and binds up their wounds.*
PSALM 147:3

Jehovah-Rophe is translated "I am the Lord thy
Physician," or "I am the Lord that healeth thee."
This name is given to reveal to us our redemptive
privilege of being healed. This privilege is purchased
by the Atonement, for Isaiah, in the Redemptive
Chapter, declares, "Surely he took up our infirmities
and carried our sorrows."

F. F. BOSWORTH

AS YOU PRAISE GOD TODAY

- Thank him that he is "the same yesterday and
  today and forever" (Hebrews 13:8). Therefore,
  he is still the Lord Who Heals.
- Pray for yourself or a loved one in need of
  physical healing, confident that Jehovah-Rophe
  is able to do it.
- Praise God for his compassion and healing.

GOD IS JEALOUS

KANNA

Do not worship any other god, for the LORD,
whose name is Jealous, is a jealous God.
EXODUS 34:14

God is not someone who can easily do without us. No, God is a jealous lover. Moses said to his people, "The LORD your God is a consuming fire, a jealous God" (Deuteronomy 4:24), and Paul said to his brothers and sisters in Corinth that he loved them with the jealous love of God (2 Corinthians 11:12). God is a lover who does not want to leave us alone for one second of our day or night. God is asking for our total, undivided attention.

HENRI J. M. NOUWEN

AS YOU PRAISE GOD TODAY

- Tell him he is your first love and there are no other gods or idols you would worship. Recognize that God is jealous for your time, your affection, and your fellowship.
- It is not a matter of large quantities of time that he wants from you. It is the quality. Put away distractions and give God your undivided attention during your times of fellowship.

GOD IS THE VOICE IN THE CLOUD

*While Aaron was speaking to the whole
Israelite community, they looked toward the desert,
and there was the glory of the LORD
appearing in the cloud.*

EXODUS 16:10

*While Peter was speaking, a cloud appeared
and enveloped them, and they were afraid
as they entered the cloud. A voice came
from the cloud, saying, "This is my Son,
whom I have chosen; listen to him."*

LUKE 9:34–35

AS YOU PRAISE GOD TODAY

- Think of your biggest problem, the issue that eats at you the most. Then focus on this: even though the situation might seem hopeless to you, God wants to somehow use it for his glory.
- Praise God that your biggest problems are small to him. Trust him to help you handle them.

GOD KNOWS
YOUR SORROWS

*The LORD, the God of their fathers, sent word
to the people of Israel through his messengers
again and again, because he had pity on his
people and on his dwelling place.*

2 CHRONICLES 36:15

*The eyes of the LORD are on the righteous
and his ears are attentive to their cry.*

PSALM 34:15

There is no thought, feeling, yearning, or desire, however low, trifling, or vulgar we may deem it, which, if it affects our real interest or happiness, we may not lay before God and be sure of his sympathy. His nature is such that our often coming does not tire him. The whole burden of the whole life of every man may be rolled onto God and not weary him, though it has wearied the man.

HENRY WARD BEECHER

AS YOU PRAISE GOD TODAY

- Thank God for opening his ears to your cry.
- No matter what you are going through, God's eyes are on you, and he knows how you feel. Praise him for being so sympathetic to your needs.

PILLAR OF FIRE

*By day the LORD went ahead of them in a pillar
of cloud to guide them on their way and by night
in a pillar of fire to give them light, so they could
travel by day or night.*

EXODUS 13:21

As [the Israelites] left Egypt, now to journey
through hostile lands, GOD took them
under His Own Care, with this visible sign of His
Guidance and Protection. It never forsook them,
till they reached the Promised Land, 40 years later.

HALLEY'S BIBLE HANDBOOK

AS YOU PRAISE GOD TODAY

- Think of the times in your life when God stood
  between you and certain disaster. Praise God for
  his intercession.
- Praise God for his wise sense of direction, guiding you only as he knows how.
- Vow to let God lead you on all your paths—he
  knows the way!

JESUS IS THE KING OF ISRAEL

Nathanael declared, "Rabbi, you are the Son of
God; you are the King of Israel."
JOHN 1:49

The great crowd that had come for the Feast
heard that Jesus was on his way to Jerusalem.
They took palm branches and went out to meet
him, shouting,
"Hosanna!"
"Blessed is he who comes in the name of the Lord!"
"Blessed is the King of Israel!"
Jesus found a young donkey and sat upon it,
as it is written,
"Do not be afraid, O Daughter of Zion;
see, your king is coming,
seated on a donkey's colt."
JOHN 12:12–15

AS YOU PRAISE GOD TODAY

- Give Jesus praise as your King who knows your heart.
- Cry out, Hosanna! Give Jesus your praise, for he comes in the name of the Lord! He *is* the Lord our king.

THE GOD OF ETERNITY

The world is firmly established;
it cannot be moved.
Your throne was established long ago;
you are from all eternity.
PSALM 93:1–2

E ternity will not be long enough to learn all he is, or to praise him for all he has done, but then, that matters not; for we shall be always with him, and we desire nothing more.

FREDERICK WILLIAM FABER

AS YOU PRAISE GOD TODAY

- Consider how amazing it is that God is an eternal being and that time knows no end with him. Worship and praise God as you ponder this amazing truth.
- Rejoice because you get to spend the rest of eternity with God!

GOD IS GRACIOUS

EL CHANUN

*The LORD passed in front of Moses, proclaiming,
"The LORD, the LORD, the compassionate and
gracious God, slow to anger, abounding in love
and faithfulness, maintaining love to thousands,
and forgiving wickedness, rebellion and sin."*

EXODUS 34:6–7

The gracious gifts of God stand every day before
your eyes whichever way you look: father and
mother, home and homestead, peace, safety, and security through worldly government, etc. Over and above
all he gave his beloved Son for you and through his
Gospel brought him home to you, to help you in every
grief and dire affliction. What more could he have
done for you, or what more or better could you wish?

MARTIN LUTHER

AS YOU PRAISE GOD TODAY

- Thank God for the mercy he has poured out on
  you (Psalm 51:1).
- Rejoice in the fact that if you accept Christ's
  sacrifice on your behalf, you will not receive the
  punishment each of us so richly deserves (Psalm
  103:1–5).

GOD IS ETERNAL

The eternal God is your refuge,
and underneath are the everlasting arms.
DEUTERONOMY 33:27

To the King eternal, immortal, invisible, the only
God, be honor and glory for ever and ever. Amen.
1 TIMOTHY 1:17

The LORD is the true God;
he is the living God, the eternal King.
JEREMIAH 10:10

You alone exist in the beginning, O God. You alone are the Alpha and Omega, the One "who is, and was, and is to come." You alone transcend and embrace even time itself.

NIV WORSHIP BIBLE

AS YOU PRAISE GOD TODAY

- God is eternal—he always has been and always will be. Glorify him with you praises.
- Rejoice in the security that God is never going anywhere; he will always be there for you.

THE NAME

<u>HASHEM</u>

*May the LORD answer you when
you are in distress;
may the name of the God of Jacob protect you.*
PSALM 20:1

*Everyone who calls
on the name of the Lord will be saved.*
ACTS 2:21

<u>AS YOU PRAISE GOD TODAY</u>

- Rejoice that you are saved by calling on God's mighty name.
- Think about that the Lord's name is far more than just a title. His name is actually his person. He is the Name.
- Thank God for placing his name on you when you were saved. Now you are his child, part of his family, and able to partake of the glory that is in his name.

JESUS IS THE KINSMAN REDEEMER

*If . . . one of your countrymen becomes poor and
sells himself to the alien living among you . . .
one of his relatives may redeem him.*

LEVITICUS 25:47–48

*Boaz said to Ruth, "Although it is true that
I am near of kin, there is a kinsman-redeemer
nearer than I. Stay here for the night, and in
the morning if he wants to redeem, good; let him
redeem. But if he is not willing, as surely as
the LORD lives I will do it."*

RUTH 3:12–13

AS YOU PRAISE GOD TODAY

- Thank god for sending Jesus to pay the ultimate
  price to free you from sin and bondage. See
  Ephesians 1:13–14.
- Praise be to the Lord, your God, because he has
  come and has redeemed his people.
- Praise him as your King and Redeemer. In him
  you have true freedom! See Isaiah 44:6–7.

GOD OF THE SPIRITS
OF ALL MANKIND

*May the LORD, the God of the spirits of all
mankind, appoint a man over this community to
go out and come in before them, one who will
lead them out and bring them in, so the LORD's
people will not be like sheep without a shepherd.*
NUMBERS 27:16–17

My spirit has become dry because it forgets to
feed on you.

JOHN OF THE CROSS

AS YOU PRAISE GOD TODAY

- Thank God that you are not just some cosmic
  accident. He created your spirit, the very essence
  of your being, and he's designed it to live forever.
- Consider that just as the body needs physical
  food to survive, your spirit needs spiritual food
  or it will wither. Nurture your spirit daily by
  reading some part of God's Word.
- Praise God for putting his spirit in your heart.

GOD LAUGHS

*The kings of the earth take their stand
and the rulers gather together
against the LORD
and against his Anointed One.
. . . The One enthroned in heaven laughs;
the LORD scoffs at them.*

PSALM 2:2, 4

*Deliver me from my enemies, O God;
protect me from those who rise up against me.
. . . See what they spew from their mouths—
they spew out swords from their lips,
and they say, "Who can hear us?"
But you, O LORD, laugh at them;
you scoff at all those nations.
. . . God will go before me
and will let me gloat over those who slander me.*

PSALM 59:1, 7–8, 10

AS YOU PRAISE GOD TODAY

- Rejoice because God always gets the last laugh.
- Praise God for coming to your aid when you need him and laughing at your enemies.

GOD IS YOUR SONG

He put a new song in my mouth,
a hymn of praise to our God.
Many will see and fear
and put their trust in the LORD.

PSALM 40:3

By day the LORD directs his love,
at night his song is with me—
a prayer to the God of my life.

PSALM 42:8

Shout for joy to the LORD, all the earth,
burst into jubilant song with music;
make music to the LORD with the harp,
with the harp and the sound of singing,

PSALM 98:4–5

AS YOU PRAISE GOD TODAY

- Sing to God a new song. Sing him songs of praise.
- Thank him for the song he has put in your heart.

GOD IS COMPASSIONATE

The LORD is gracious and righteous;
our God is full of compassion.
PSALM 116:5

I will betroth you to me forever . . .
in love and compassion
EXODUS 34:6–7

The Old Testament tells the story of God's marriage to his people. The most notable characteristic of this marriage is the unfaithfulness of the bride and the passionate, tortured response of the Husband. If you consider the entire Bible, you cannot help but see that despite God's passionate anger and jealousy, it is his love and humility that dominate. At the slightest sign of repentance, he throws his arms open to his bride once again. Hope persistently rises in the background.

TIM STAFFORD

AS YOU PRAISE GOD TODAY

- Meditate on Exodus 34:6–7, and pray it for yourself. Marvel at his compassionate and forgiving nature, and praise him for it.

THE LORD IS ONE

Hear, O Israel: The LORD our God,
the LORD is one.
DEUTERONOMY 6:4

There is one body and one Spirit—just as you
were called to one hope when you were called—
one Lord, one faith, one baptism; one God
and Father of all, who is over all and through
all and in all.
EPHESIANS 4:4–6

AS YOU PRAISE GOD TODAY

- Meditate on the wonderful mystery that he is one God in three Persons.
- Praise him that he is the only One, True God.
- Give thanks for the One God, Father over all.

GOD IS FAITHFUL

Great is your love, higher than the heavens;
your faithfulness reaches to the skies.
Be exalted, O God, above the heavens,
and let your glory be over all the earth.
PSALM 108:4–5

Pastor Bill Hybels tells of a time when he was asked to speak to a large gathering in India. His inexperience and fear of failure had almost immobilized him, but then he made "a faithful God" the object of his attention: "I'm praying to the Creator of the world, the King of the universe, the all-powerful, all-knowing, all-faithful God. I'm praying to the God who has always been faithful to me, who has never let me down no matter how frightened I was or how difficult the situation looked. I am going to trust that he is going to use me tonight. Not because of who I am, but because of who he is. He is faithful."

AS YOU PRAISE GOD TODAY

- Praise God for the many ways he has proven himself faithful in your life.
- Rejoice that God is always faithful even when we are not.
- Praise him for standing by you when you needed him most.

GOD IS GREAT

The LORD your God is God of gods and LORD of lords, the great God, mighty and awesome, who shows no partiality and accepts no bribes.

DEUTERONOMY 10:17

There are times that God cannot reveal himself in any other way than in his majesty, and it is the awesomeness of the vision which brings you to the delight of despair. You experience this joy in hopelessness, realizing that if you are ever to be raised up it must be by the hand of God.

God can do nothing for me until I recognize the limits of what is humanly possible, allowing him to do the impossible.

OSWALD CHAMBERS

AS YOU PRAISE GOD TODAY

- Praise God for being the Almighty God who can do the impossible in your life!
- As you pray, describe God with adjectives such as great, awesome, all-powerful, mighty, and supreme.

GOD OF GODS

ELOHAY ELOHIM

Who among the gods is like you, O LORD?
Who is like you—majestic in holiness, awesome
in glory, working wonders?
EXODUS 15:11

Let us come before him with thanksgiving
and extol him with music and song.
For the LORD is the great God,
the great King above all gods.
In his hand are the depths of the earth,
and the mountain peaks belong to him.
PSALM 95:2–4

AS YOU PRAISE GOD TODAY

- Rejoice that in One Being, above all others, he is power, wisdom, peace and love.
- Praise God that he, the only true God, has revealed himself to you.
- As you pray, give him thanks for being greater than anything you can imagine.

GOD IS MERCIFUL

*Jesus said, "Be merciful, just as your
Father is merciful."*
LUKE 6:36

The Lord called Jonah to deliver a message of repentance to Ninevah, but Jonah didn't answer the call. In fact, Jonah ran away. But the Bible tells us that the Lord called again. This time, after a ride in a fish's belly, Jonah cooperated. He followed God's call, and Ninevah repented. God gave Jonah a second chance that ultimately saved a city. Is there someone in your church that deserves a second chance? A second chance may be just what's needed to follow God's plan, rescue a relationship, or even make a new friend.

SARAH M. HUPP

AS YOU PRAISE GOD TODAY

- Give thanks to God for his compassion when you have struggled against his will for you.
- Praise him and give thanks for the times God has given you a second chance.
- Praise God for with his perfect justice he offers mercy.

GOD IS OMNISCIENT

Great is our LORD and mighty in power;
his understanding has no limit.
PSALM 147:5

The eyes of the LORD are everywhere,
keeping watch on the wicked and the good.
PROVERBS 15:3

"Who has known the mind of the Lord
that he may instruct him?"
But we have the mind of Christ.
1 CORINTHIANS 2:16

AS YOU PRAISE GOD TODAY

- Think about 1 Corinthians 2:16 above and rejoice that God has given you the mind of Christ.
- Praise God that nothing goes on in this world that he does not know. Praise his holy name!

GOD IS WISE

*To the only wise God be glory forever through
Jesus Christ! Amen.*
ROMANS 16:27

*Oh, the depth of the riches of the wisdom
and knowledge of God!
How unsearchable his judgments,
and his paths beyond tracing out!*
ROMANS 11:33

As a blind man has no idea of colors, so have we
no idea of the manner by which the all-wise
God perceives and understands all things.

SIR ISAAC NEWTON

AS YOU PRAISE GOD TODAY

- Consider the quote above and praise God for
  being an all-wise God, whose wisdom has no end.
- Consider that the foolishness of God is wiser
  than your human wisdom. Give God praise for
  making his wisdom known through his Word.

GOD OF THE BEGINNING

ELOHAY KEDEM

*In the beginning God created
the heavens and the earth.*
GENESIS 1:1

The God of the Beginning is the Powerful One who is before all things in time and priority. God was there in the beginning of time, in the beginning of creation, in the beginning of Jesus' life on earth, in the beginning of Jesus' reign in heaven, in the beginning of the church, in the beginning of your life and every event in your life. He deserves our attention at the beginning of every day and our fellowship at the beginning of every week. He must be first, before all else.

AS YOU PRAISE GOD TODAY

- Give God praise at the beginning of each day, declaring he is Lord over your day.
- Praise him as the God who has been with you for all of the beginnings in your life.
- Praise God for being the ultimate power who alone can bring about all he has promised, from the beginning of the world to the end.

GOD IS YOUR HELPER

We say with confidence,
"The Lord is my helper; I will not be afraid.
What can man do to me?"
HEBREWS 13:6

The LORD is with me; he is my helper.
I will look in triumph on my enemies.
PSALM 118:7

You, O God, do see trouble and grief;
you consider it to take it in hand.
The victim commits himself to you;
you are the helper of the fatherless.
PSALM 10:14

AS YOU PRAISE GOD TODAY

- Thank God for his promise that no matter what you face in life, he has committed himself to be your helper.
- Rejoice that with God as your helper, nothing and no one can stand against you.

THE LORD OF ARMIES

JEHOVAH-TZ'VAOT

When Joshua was near Jericho, he looked up and
saw a man standing in front of him with a
drawn sword in his hand. Joshua went up to him
and asked, "Are you for us or for our enemies?"
"Neither," he replied, "but as commander of the
army of the LORD I have now come."

JOSHUA 5:13–14

The Lord of Armies is the most powerful being and the greatest warrior in the universe. God is the general of his armies in heaven and on earth. He is the Supreme Commander in Chief. You can rest in his hands, sure that he will fight for you and win the victory.

AS YOU PRAISE GOD TODAY

- Thank God for the security you can feel in the care of the Chief Commander of the heavenly hosts.
- Rejoice that you know how the war ends—the army of God has the victory already, and the Commander is God Almighty!

THE SPIRIT OF THE LORD

Samuel took the horn of oil and anointed him
in the presence of his brothers, and from
that day on the Spirit of the LORD
came upon David in power.

1 SAMUEL 16:13

Since, Lord, thou dost defend
Us with thy Spirit,
We know we at the end
Shall life inherit.
Then fancies, flee away!
I'll fear not what men say;
I'll labor night and day
To be a pilgrim.

C. WINFRED DOUGLAS

AS YOU PRAISE GOD TODAY

- Praise God for giving you something stronger than the strongest weapon: his Spirit.
- Praise him that he doesn't give his Spirit to the oldest, or the strongest, or the best-looking. God gives his Spirit to all those who believe in him, no matter how weak or lowly they may be.

THE GOD OF THE COVENANT

EL BERITH

O LORD, God of Israel, there is no God like you in heaven or on earth—you who keep your covenant of love with your servants who continue wholeheartedly in your way.

2 CHRONICLES 6:14

You know that the promises of God are there . . . Do you still respond, "But it seems so unlikely that my poor, helpless soul should be sustained by such strength." . . . If God has said so, surely you do not want to suggest he has lied! . . . If he has given you his word—his sure word of promise—do not question it but trust it absolutely. You have his promise, and in fact you have even more—you have him who confidently speaks the words.

J. B. FIGGIS

AS YOU PRAISE GOD TODAY

- Read these Scriptures that speak of God's unalterable covenant: Psalm 89:34; Exodus 6:5; Isaiah 54:10; Romans 11:26–27.
- Rejoice that God establishes his covenant promise with his people, never to be broken.

GOD IS PERFECT IN KNOWLEDGE

By wisdom the LORD laid the earth's foundations,
by understanding he set the heavens in place;
by his knowledge the deeps were divided,
and the clouds let drop the dew.

PROVERBS 3:19–20

The earth will be full of the knowledge of the LORD
as the waters cover the sea.

ISAIAH 11:9

The more we learn about the wonders of our universe, the more clearly we are going to perceive the hand of God.

FRANK BORMAN

AS YOU PRAISE GOD TODAY

- Think about the wonder of God's knowledge and how it affects you.
- Praise him for how amazing his knowledge is.
- Ask God to reveal to you more wonderful things about his knowledge.

GOD KNOWS YOU

*O LORD, you have searched me
and you know me.
You know when I sit and when I rise;
you perceive my thoughts from afar.
You discern my going out and my lying down;
you are familiar with all my ways.*

PSALM 139:1–3

God does not simply note your actions; he does not simply notice what the appearance of your countenance is. God sees what you are thinking of; he looks within. He does not want you to tell him what you are thinking about—he can see that. He can read right through you. He knows every thought, every imagination, every conception. He even knows unformed imagination—the thought scarcely shot from the bow, reserved in the quiver of the mind. He sees it all, every particle, every atom of it.

CHARLES H. SPURGEON

AS YOU PRAISE GOD TODAY

- Thank God for knowing you better than you know yourself.
- Praise him for being intimately acquainted with everything that concerns you.

GOD IS YOUR DELIVERER

PALET

*"Call upon me in the day of trouble;
I will deliver you, and you will honor me."*
PSALM 50:15

Do not look forward to the changes and chances of this life in fear; rather look to them with full hope that, as they arise, God, whose you are, will deliver you out of them. He is your Keeper. He has kept you hitherto. Hold fast to his dear hand, and he will lead you safely through all things; and, when you cannot stand, he will bear you in his arms. Do not look forward to what may happen tomorrow. Our Father will either shield you from suffering, or he will give you strength to bear it.

SAINT FRANCIS OF SALES

AS YOU PRAISE GOD TODAY

- Praise God for his mighty delivering power. He was able to deliver the children of Israel from all their enemies and assures you that he will do the same for you.

GOD IS YOUR STRONGHOLD

The LORD is my rock, my fortress and my deliverer;
my God is my rock, in whom I take refuge.
He is my shield and the horn of my salvation,
my stronghold.
I call to the LORD, who is worthy of praise,
and I am saved from my enemies.

PSALM 18:2–3

God's power is infinitely greater than the military might of any nation. Our modern-day enemies may not wage war with swords, but perhaps they launch their attacks with threats or persecution or in a variety of more subtle ways.

Our most vicious enemy, Satan, is ultimately responsible for every spiritual assault, whether it manifests itself physically, emotionally, or through seemingly coincidental circumstances. When it seems that a political, social, or spiritual enemy is stronger than we are, we can remember that God's promise of safety and protection is absolutely trustworthy.

LIFE PROMISES BIBLE

AS YOU PRAISE GOD TODAY

- Praise God and give him thanks that his protection is available anytime you call out to him.

GOD IS YOUR ROCK

ELOHAY TZUR

Trust in the LORD forever,
for the LORD, the LORD, is the Rock eternal.
ISAIAH 26:4

The LORD lives! Praise be to my Rock!
Exalted be God, the Rock, my Savior!
2 SAMUEL 22:47

Come, let us sing for joy to the LORD;
let us shout aloud to the Rock of our salvation.
Let us come before him with thanksgiving
and extol him with music and song.
PSALM 95:1–2

AS YOU PRAISE GOD TODAY

- Think of all the ways he has shown himself to be a Rock in your life and give him praise.
- Thank God for being your rock when you need a place of refuge. You can run to him and be safe because God is an immovable rock to which you can always cling.

THE LORD OF HOSTS

JEHOVAH-SABAOTH

*I saw heaven standing open and there before me
was a white horse, whose rider is called Faithful
and True. With justice he judges and makes war.
His eyes are like blazing fire, and on his head are
many crowns. He has a name written on him
that no one knows but he himself. He is dressed
in a robe dipped in blood, and his name is
the Word of God. The armies of heaven were
following him, riding on white horses and dressed
in fine linen, white and clean.*

REVELATION 19:11–14

AS YOU PRAISE GOD TODAY

- Praise him for being a victorious warrior, the Lord of all the hosts of heaven.
- Reflect on the fact that although you cannot see them, there is an entire host of angels ready to fight on your behalf.
- Thank God that as part of his army, you are also victorious.

GOD IS THE ONLY
TRUE GOD

"I am the LORD, and there is no other;
apart from me there is no God.
I will strengthen you,
though you have not acknowledged me,
so that from the rising of the sun
to the place of its setting
men may know there is none besides me.
I am the LORD, and there is no other."

ISAIAH 45:5–6

Jesus said, "This is eternal life: that they may
know you, the only true God, and Jesus Christ,
whom you have sent."

JOHN 17:3

AS YOU PRAISE GOD TODAY

- Think about how inferior all other gods are
  compared to him; the One true God.
- Thank God for showing you the truth that he is
  the only true God.

THE GOD OF HEAVEN AND EARTH

ELAH SH'MAYA V'ARAH

*Yours, O LORD, is the greatness and the power
and the glory and the majesty and the splendor,
for everything in heaven and earth is yours.
Yours, O LORD, is the kingdom;
you are exalted as head over all.
Wealth and honor come from you;
you are the ruler of all things.
In your hands are strength and power
to exalt and give strength to all.
Now, our God, we give you thanks,
and praise your glorious name.*

1 CHRONICLES 29:11–13

AS YOU PRAISE GOD TODAY

- Rejoice in his power and majesty as the Lord of heaven and earth.
- Think about how God owns everything on earth and in heaven—even your car, your house, your income. It's all his and he lets you use it. Thank him for his generosity!

THE GOD OF BATTLES

*Do not be afraid. Stand firm and you will see the
deliverance the LORD will bring you today. The
Egyptians you see today you will never see again. The
LORD will fight for you; you need only to be still.*

EXODUS 14:13–14

We are soldiers of the light. He has given us his
light; he has given us his sword; he has given us
his name. Allow him to shine through you. Wield the
laser sword of the Spirit. How destructive to darkness
is his lightning sword. Station yourself spiritually in
front of your rebellious children and ask God to send
a bolt of meekness to them. Aim the light of liberty at
their addictions, whether drugs, sex, alcohol, or whatever. Ask God to shine forth, breaking through the
darkness of deception. As the Israelites carried the
presence and glory of God into battle, so must we.

DUTCH SHEETS

AS YOU PRAISE GOD TODAY

- Praise God for his willingness to fight your
  battles.
- Thank him that you do not have to be afraid
  because he fights for you.

THE GOD OF JERUSALEM

ELAH YERUSH'LEM

Jesus said: "Him who overcomes I will make a pillar in the temple of my God. Never again will he leave it. I will write on him the name of my God and the name of the city of my God, the new Jerusalem, which is coming down out of heaven from my God; and I will also write on him my new name."

REVELATION 3:12

The Holy City of Your presence is the fortress of my life. I will remain in that fortress until the time You have appointed for my residence in the new Jerusalem—where there will be no more death or mourning or crying or pain. Your works are glorious, and in Your presence there is joy forever!

NIV WORSHIP BIBLE

AS YOU PRAISE GOD TODAY

- Think about the city of New Jerusalem, your home for the rest of eternity.
- Praise God for preparing a home for you, the home that you've always yearned for but have not yet seen.

THE GOD OF ISRAEL

ELAH YISRAEL

You are awesome, O God, in your sanctuary;
the God of Israel gives power
and strength to his people.
PSALM 68:35

Praise be to the LORD God, the God of Israel,
who alone does marvelous deeds.
Praise be to his glorious name forever;
may the whole earth be filled with his glory.
PSALM 72:18–19

The God of Israel is the Lord who fights battles for his people, the Lord who speaks to his people, the Lord who reveals himself and his mysteries to his people, the Lord who helps his people and gives them strength. All his acts are loving toward his people. The God of Israel is to be praised!

AS YOU PRAISE GOD TODAY

- Read the verses on this page and think about what they reveal about God.
- Thank God for all he does for you—you are also part of his people through salvation in Jesus.

GOD OF HEAVEN

ELAH SH'MAYA

Give thanks to the God of heaven.
His love endures forever.
PSALM 136:26

Praise be to the name of God for ever and ever;
wisdom and power are his.
He changes times and seasons;
he sets up kings and deposes them.
He gives wisdom to the wise
and knowledge to the discerning.
He reveals deep and hidden things;
he knows what lies in darkness,
and light dwells with him.
DANIEL 2:19–22

AS YOU PRAISE GOD TODAY

- As in Psalm 136:26 above, give thanks to God because his mercy endures forever.
- Praise God for changing the times and seasons, setting up kings, giving wisdom and knowledge, and revealing deep and hidden things.

GOD IS YOUR REDEEMER

GAOL

"I have swept away your offenses like a cloud,
your sins like the morning mist.
Return to me,
for I have redeemed you."
Sing for joy, O heavens, for the LORD has done this;
shout aloud, O earth beneath.
Burst into song, you mountains,
you forests and all your trees,
for the LORD has redeemed Jacob,
he displays his glory in Israel.
ISAIAH 44:22–23

"I am the LORD, and I will bring you out from
under the yoke of the Egyptians. I will free you
from being slaves to them, and I will redeem you
with an outstretched arm and with mighty acts
of judgment. I will take you as my own people,
and I will be your God."
EXODUS 6:6–7

AS YOU PRAISE GOD TODAY

- Look up the definition of the word "redeem" and praise God that this word applies to you!
- Read Job 19:25 and rejoice because your Redeemer lives!

GOD IS YOUR SHIELD

MAGAN

We wait in hope for the LORD;
he is our help and our shield.
In him our hearts rejoice,
for we trust in his holy name.
PSALM 33:20–21

In battle the shield, thrust out in front of the warrior, protects him from the enemy's arrows, spears, swords, and fists. The image of God as protector or sovereign must have been a great comfort to David, and we can take comfort in this promise today as well. However the devil, our great adversary, approaches us, God is in control and will shield us from his deathblows. If we rely on God's protection and keep our shield in place—directly in front of us and over the heart—he will cast out our fears.

LIFE PROMISES BIBLE

AS YOU PRAISE GOD TODAY

- Praise God for placing his shield around you and protecting you from the arrows of the enemy.
- Think of all the ways God is a shield in your life. Thank God for being your protective shield.

GOD IS YOUR LORD
AND KING

Even the sparrow has found a home,
and the swallow a nest for herself,
where she may have her young—
a place near your altar,
O LORD Almighty, my King and my God.
Blessed are those who dwell in your house;
they are ever praising you.

PSALM 84:3–4

Your procession has come into view, O God,
the procession of my God and King
into the sanctuary.
In front are the singers, after them the musicians;
with them are the maidens playing tambourines.
Praise God in the great congregation;
praise the LORD in the assembly of Israel.

PSALM 68:24–26

AS YOU PRAISE GOD TODAY

- Think about how he is *your* Lord and King. He
  even declares himself to be your God. Give God
  praise and glory for making his relationship with
  you personal.

GOD IS THE RIGHTEOUS ONE

TSADDIQ

*"There is no God apart from me,
a righteous God and a Savior;
there is none but me."*
ISAIAH 45:21

*The LORD is righteous in all his ways
and loving toward all he has made.*
PSALM 145:17

*It is because of God that you are in Christ Jesus,
who has become for us wisdom from God—that
is, our righteousness, holiness and redemption.*
1 CORINTHIANS 1:30

AS YOU PRAISE GOD TODAY

- Praise him for being righteous in all his ways.
  God cannot be unrighteous, so you can fully
  trust him.
- Praise God that he is righteous and through his
  Son he has made you righteous, too.

GOD SEARCHES YOUR HEART

The LORD searches every heart and understands every motive behind the thoughts. If you seek him, he will be found by you.

1 CHRONICLES 28:9

[God] who searches our hearts knows the mind of the Spirit, because the Spirit intercedes for the saints in accordance with God's will.

ROMANS 8:27

If you ... begin to find that the Holy Spirit is scrutinizing you, let his searchlight go straight down, and he will not only search you, he will put everything right that is wrong; he will make the past as though it had never been.

OSWALD CHAMBERS

AS YOU PRAISE GOD TODAY

- Rejoice that God cares enough for you to search your heart.
- Thank God that the reason he searches and examines you is to reward you and to put everything right that is wrong. You truly are blessed by God!

THE GOD WHO DOES ALL THINGS RIGHT

"I, the LORD, speak the truth;
I declare what is right."
ISAIAH 45:19

Good and upright is the LORD;
therefore he instructs sinners in his ways.
He guides the humble in what is right
and teaches them his way.
PSALM 25:8–9

Sovereign Lord, You are the Almighty Creator, the Holy and Righteous One. You are the Eternal Father, the infinite source of all life. In Your Presence are truth and wisdom. Righteousness and justice surround Your throne. I worship You, my God and Father, with reverence and awe.

NIV WORSHIP BIBLE

AS YOU PRAISE GOD TODAY

- Praise God for being everything that is pure and true and right.
- Rejoice that he makes all things right.
- Thank God for guiding you in what is right.

GOD IS YOUR INHERITANCE

LORD, you have assigned me my portion
and my cup;
you have made my lot secure.
The boundary lines have fallen for me in
pleasant places;
surely I have a delightful inheritance.

PSALM 16:5–6

My flesh and my heart may fail,
but God is the strength of my heart
and my portion forever.

PSALM 73:26

God is the everlasting portion of his people. When a man born from above begins his new life, he meets God at every turn, hears him in every sound, sleeps at his feet, and wakes to find him there.

OSWALD CHAMBERS

AS YOU PRAISE GOD TODAY

- Rejoice that in all his glory, God is your portion forever.
- Thank him for the Holy Spirit who is the guarantee of your inheritance.

GOD IS KIND

"With everlasting kindness
I will have compassion on you,"
says the LORD your Redeemer.
ISAIAH 54:8

I will tell of the kindnesses of the LORD,
the deeds for which he is to be praised,
according to all the LORD has done for us—
yes, the many good things he has done
for the house of Israel,
according to his compassion and many kindnesses.
ISAIAH 63:7

When the kindness and love of God our Savior
appeared, he saved us, not because of righteous
things we had done, but because of his mercy.
TITUS 3:4–5

AS YOU PRAISE GOD TODAY

- Rejoice that he is kind.
- Praise God for the ways in which he has been kind to you.

GOD IS YOUR SAVIOR

"There is no God apart from me,
a righteous God and a Savior;
there is none but me."
ISAIAH 45:21

"He will call upon me, and I will answer him;
I will be with him in trouble,
I will deliver him and honor him.
With long life will I satisfy him
and show him my salvation."
PSALM 91:15–16

To the only God our Savior be glory,
majesty, power and authority, through
Jesus Christ our Lord, before all ages,
now and forevermore! Amen.
JUDE 25

AS YOU PRAISE GOD TODAY

- Thank him for sending Jesus to save you!
- Rejoice in all the ways God saves you daily.

GOD IS YOUR STRENGTH

EYALUTH

I thank Christ Jesus our Lord, who has given me strength, that he considered me faithful, appointing me to his service.

1 TIMOTHY 1:12

Here is the answer to stress, regardless of its origin, nature, or intensity: Let the pressure drive you to the Source of all your strength, peace, and stability—the Person of Jesus Christ. The apostle Paul came to that wise conclusion after considering the many hardships he endured: "But this happened, that we might not rely on ourselves but on God" (2 Corinthians 1:9).

CHARLES STANLEY

AS YOU PRAISE GOD TODAY

- Praise him for being your strength in times of weakness.
- Thank him for giving you the strength to do what he has called you to do.

JESUS IS YOUR SHEPHERD

*Jesus said, "I am the good shepherd. The good
shepherd lays down his life for the sheep."*
JOHN 10:11

*Jesus said, "I am the good shepherd; I know my
sheep and my sheep know me—just as the Father
knows me and I know the Father—and I lay
down my life for the sheep."*
JOHN 10:14–15

Christ the Creator of such an enormous universe
of overwhelming magnitude, deigns to call Himself my Shepherd and invites me to consider myself
His sheep—His special object of affection and attention. Who better could care for me?

PHILLIP KELLER

AS YOU PRAISE GOD TODAY

- Thank Jesus for calling you into his fold and for
being such a wonderful shepherd to you.
- Read 1 Peter 2:25 and Revelation 7:17 about
Jesus being your shepherd, and give him praise.

GOD IS YOUR GUIDE

The LORD will guide you always;
he will satisfy your needs in a sun-scorched land
and will strengthen your frame.
You will be like a well-watered garden,
like a spring whose waters never fail.

ISAIAH 58:11

The Lord leads us both in life and in death. He guides all our days, up to and beyond the moment we draw our last earthly breath. We can trust in God always to be our confidant and guide, whether on earth or in heaven. "You guide me with your counsel, and afterward you will take me into glory" (Psalms 73:24).

LIFE PROMISES BIBLE

AS YOU PRAISE GOD TODAY

- Praise God for being a faithful guide to you at all times.
- Thank him for guiding you on the path he has chosen for you.

GOD IS YOUR LIGHT

Though I sit in darkness,
the LORD will be my light.
MICAH 7:8

The sun will no more be your light by day,
nor will the brightness of the moon shine on you,
for the LORD will be your everlasting light,
and your God will be your glory.
ISAIAH 60:19

God is light; in him there is no darkness at all.
1 JOHN 1:5

AS YOU PRAISE GOD TODAY

- Think of ways God's light has helped you see spiritual things more clearly.
- Praise him for being your light and for dispelling all darkness.

GOD OF GLORY

EL HAKAVOD

Ascribe to the LORD, O mighty ones,
ascribe to the LORD glory and strength.
Ascribe to the LORD the glory due his name;
worship the LORD in the splendor of his holiness.
The voice of the LORD is over the waters;
the God of glory thunders,
the LORD thunders over the mighty waters.
The voice of the LORD is powerful;
the voice of the LORD is majestic.

PSALM 29:1–4

AS YOU PRAISE GOD TODAY

• Worship him as the God, King, and Lord of Glory. Praise God for revealing his glory to you.

THE GOD OF TRUTH

EL EMET

Into your hands I commit my spirit;
redeem me, O LORD, the God of truth.
PSALM 31:5

"I, the LORD, speak the truth;
I declare what is right."
ISAIAH 45:19

The Son of God has come and has given us
understanding, so that we may know him
who is true. And we are in him who is true—
even in his Son Jesus Christ. He is the true
God and eternal life.
1 JOHN 5:20

AS YOU PRAISE GOD TODAY

- Praise God that he is not "a truth," or "truth for me," or "truth for you," but he is the absolute truth for everyone everywhere.
- Praise God that all lies, all secret cheats, will some day be fully exposed under the blazing light of his truth.

GOD IS MY HIDING PLACE

You are my hiding place;
you will protect me from trouble
and surround me with songs of deliverance.

PSALM 32:7

In the day of trouble
he will keep me safe in his dwelling;
he will hide me in the shelter of his tabernacle
and set me high upon a rock.

PSALM 27:5

AS YOU PRAISE GOD TODAY

- Thank God for the many times he has sheltered you from harm.
- Praise him for being an ever-present hiding place to which you can run at any time.
- Rejoice that God's hiding place is impenetrable by any power of the enemy.

GOD IS LOVE

*We know and rely on the love God has for us.
God is love. Whoever lives in love lives in God,
and God in him.*

1 JOHN 4:16

*I will sing of the LORD's great love forever;
with my mouth I will make your faithfulness
known through all generations.
I will declare that your love stands firm forever,
that you established your faithfulness in heaven itself.*

PSALM 89:1–2

*O Love that will not let me go,
I rest my weary soul in Thee,
I give Thee back the life I owe,
That in thine ocean depths its flow
May richer, fuller be.*

GEORGE MATHESON

AS YOU PRAISE GOD TODAY

- Praise God for the vastness and unending faithfulness of his love for you.
- Praise him that his love has conquered sin and death.
- Worship God for loving you enough to send his only Son to save you.

GOD OF YOUR LIFE

EL CHAIYAI

By day the LORD directs his love,
at night his song is with me—
a prayer to the God of my life.

PSALM 42:8

You crafted me into a new creation full of divine purpose and value. I have been transformed from death to life, from hopelessness to purposefulness, from ashes to beauty, and all by the prerogative of Your grace. What can I do in response but to thank You for living in me and to seek with all my heart to live in You?

NIV WORSHIP BIBLE

AS YOU PRAISE GOD TODAY

- Praise God that he is what life is all about, and he has allowed you to know him personally.
- Ponder the many ways God's life has impacted and affected your life.
- Praise God for the gift of life in Jesus.

GOD IS YOUR ROCK

EL SALI

*The LORD is my rock, my fortress
and my deliverer;
my God is my rock, in whom I take refuge.*
PSALM 18:2

*Be my rock of refuge,
to which I can always go;
give the command to save me,
for you are my rock and my fortress.*
PSALM 71:3

*Rock of Ages, cleft for me,
Let me hide myself in thee.*
AUGUSTUS MONTAGUE TOPLADY

AS YOU PRAISE GOD TODAY

- Praise God for being your rock, your fortress and stronghold. Though the world changes constantly around you, God will not be moved and you can run to him for shelter.
- Praise God that your belief in him is not based on your feelings but on his character, which is solid as a rock.

GOD IS YOUR PEACE

The Apostle Paul wrote, "Whatever you have
learned or received or heard from me, or seen
in me—put it into practice. And the God of
peace will be with you."

PHILIPPIANS 4:9

When you mention the word "peace" people visibly relax. The traditional Jewish greeting is shalom, meaning "peace"—a wish for completeness and well-being that can only come from God. An aspect of God's nature, peace carries with it the ideas of security, contentment, prosperity, and end to strife. When you immerse yourself in God's peace, it is as if your spirit relaxes in a gently swaying hammock of safety, refreshed in the balmy breezes of tranquillity. Have you ever felt this kind of peace? Do you want to experience it more often? Get to know the God of peace.

SARAH M. HUPP

AS YOU PRAISE GOD TODAY

- Rejoice that he is also the God peace! Partake of God's peace today.
- Praise God for equipping you with everything you need to do his will.

GOD IS THE JOY OF YOUR EXALTATION

EL SIMCHAT GILI

You have made known to me the path of life;
you will fill me with joy in your presence,
with eternal pleasures at your right hand.

PSALM 16:11

Do not grieve, for the joy of
the LORD is your strength.

NEHEMIAH 8:10

I have no understanding of a long-faced Christian.
If God is anything, he must be joy.

JOE E. BROWN

AS YOU PRAISE GOD TODAY

- Praise God for being the only source of lasting joy—the joy than endures regardless of circumstances.
- Rejoice that he chose to have a relationship with you!
- Praise God for all the ways he's blessed you. Remember not only the big things, but also the countless little things that are so easily forgotten.

GOD IS YOUR REFUGE

God is our refuge and strength,
an ever-present help in trouble.
PSALM 46:1

God is your refuge, your place of rest and refreshment in the thick of hardship. Unlike others who often turn us away during our time of trouble, God actually invites us to step into his safety and protection. We can run into the arms of God and find a hiding place where our emotions and spirits are nurtured. David's long, harrowing years of fleeing from Saul found him crying out often for God to be his stronghold, his rock, his defense, his fortress, his refuge. The young shepherd depended on God, not the rugged terrain of Israel, to shelter him.

CHARLES STANLEY

AS YOU PRAISE GOD TODAY

- Read Psalm 18.
- Think of one stressful thing in your life that you can give to God and run to his arms for refuge.
- Rejoice that God is your refuge and you can run to him whenever you need a place of safety.

GOD SPEAKS IN A STILL, SMALL VOICE

After the earthquake came a fire,
but the LORD was not in the fire.
And after the fire came a gentle whisper.

1 KINGS 19:12

God's presence and voice came to an exhausted Elijah in a "gentle whisper," not in the thunderous roar of earthquake, hurricane, and fire. The awesome God who had split rocks and parted seas came to Elijah on a gentle breeze, soft but still rich enough with holy majesty that Elijah reverently wrapped his cloak across his face as God spoke to him (1 Kings 19:11–13). God comes to us as a gentleman. He doesn't shout. Our soul and mind need to be uncluttered and stilled so we can hear him.

CHARLES STANLEY

AS YOU PRAISE GOD TODAY

- Praise God that although he is almighty God, bigger than you could ever imagine, he chooses to speak softly to you.
- Write down the thoughts and/or Scriptures that come to mind as you wait quietly on the Lord. These impressions are his still, small voice speaking to you.

GOD IS THE KING OF ALL THE EARTH

O LORD Almighty, God of Israel, enthroned between the cherubim, you alone are God over all the kingdoms of the earth. You have made heaven and earth.

ISAIAH 37:16

Clap your hands, all you nations;
shout to God with cries of joy.
How awesome is the LORD Most High,
the great King over all the earth! . . .
God is the King of all the earth;
sing to him a psalm of praise.
God reigns over the nations;
God is seated on his holy throne.
The nobles of the nations assemble
as the people of the God of Abraham,
for the kings of the earth belong to God;
he is greatly exalted.

PSALM 47:1–2, 7–9

AS YOU PRAISE GOD TODAY

- Praise God for being the King of All the Earth, who knows all that is taking place on the earth. Praise him and greatly exalt him in this role.
- Praise God for having his way in the kingdoms of this earth.

GOD IS YOUR MAKER

Rich and poor have this in common:
The LORD is the Maker of them all.
PROVERBS 22:2

You created my inmost being;
you knit me together in my mother's womb.
I praise you because I am fearfully
and wonderfully made;
your works are wonderful,
I know that full well.
My frame was not hidden from you
when I was made in the secret place.
When I was woven together in the depths
of the earth,
your eyes saw my unformed body.
All the days ordained for me
were written in your book
before one of them came to be.
PSALM 139:13–16

AS YOU PRAISE GOD TODAY

- Praise God that he has a magnificent, detailed plan for you, even though you can't yet see what it is.
- Praise him for making you the way you are.

THE HOLY SPIRIT

*Jesus said, "The Counselor, the Holy Spirit,
whom the Father will send in my name,
will teach you all things and will remind you
of everything I have said to you."*
JOHN 14:26

*Repent and be baptized, every one of you,
in the name of Jesus Christ for the forgiveness
of your sins. And you will receive the gift
of the Holy Spirit.*
ACTS 2:38

AS YOU PRAISE GOD TODAY

- Thank God for the gift of the Holy Spirit, who is our comforter and companion.
- Read the Scriptures on this page and meditate on the fact that the Holy Spirit is a Person, not a thing or an "it" as some have thought.
- Realize that you carry this precious gift within you everywhere you go—the Spirit of God. You can talk to God at all times; he lives within you, directing your steps and protecting you.

GOD IS A TOWER OF STRENGTH

*You have been my refuge,
a strong tower against the foe.*
PSALM 61:3

*The name of the LORD is a strong tower;
the righteous run to it and are safe.*
PROVERBS 18:10

For Solomon, the name of the Lord was (and is) a strong tower. His name didn't *mean* strong tower; he *was* a strong tower, a place where the righteous could find safety and protection. To say that Yahweh (God's given name; see Exodus 3:14–15) is my God is to say that my God is a tower of safety and strength.

LIFE PROMISES BIBLE

AS YOU PRAISE GOD TODAY

- Praise God for being a tall and strong tower. If you trust in him, you will be protected from the enemy and see the enemy from far away, so he can never surprise you.
- Praise Jesus for letting you into his tower.

GOD IS CHANGELESS

*Jesus Christ is the same yesterday
and today and forever.*
HEBREWS 13:8

I the LORD do not change .
MALACHI 3:6

*In the beginning, O Lord, you laid
the foundations of the earth,
and the heavens are the work of your hands.
They will perish, but you remain;
they will all wear out like a garment.
You will roll them up like a robe;
like a garment they will be changed.
But you remain the same,
and your years will never end.*
HEBREWS 1:10–12

AS YOU PRAISE GOD TODAY

- Praise God for being the One you can count on to always stay the same.
- Think of all the ways this brings stability to your life, and give him praise.

HOLY ONE OF ISRAEL

Blessed are those who have learned to acclaim you,
who walk in the light of your presence, O LORD.
They rejoice in your name all day long;
they exult in your righteousness.
For you are their glory and strength,
and by your favor you exalt our horn.
Indeed, our shield belongs to the LORD,
our king to the Holy One of Israel.
PSALM 89:15–18

"The Holy One of Israel" (Psalm 89:18) will defend and deliver his own. We can be sure that his every word will stand forever, even though the mountains may fall into the sea. He deserves our total confidence. So come, my soul, return to your place of peace, and rest within the sweet embrace of the Lord Jesus.

MRS. CHARLES E. COWMAN

AS YOU PRAISE GOD TODAY

- Look up the definition of "holy" and think about the many ways that God is holy.
- This name is majestic and powerful. In what other ways does this name fit your perception of who God is?
- Pray for more understanding of God's holiness.

GOD IS BEAUTIFUL

In that day the LORD Almighty
will be a glorious crown,
a beautiful wreath
for the remnant of his people.
ISAIAH 28:5

One thing I ask of the LORD,
this is what I seek:
that I may dwell in the house of the LORD
all the days of my life,
to gaze upon the beauty of the LORD
and to seek him in his temple. . . .
at his tabernacle will I sacrifice with shouts of joy;
I will sing and make music to the LORD.
PSALM 27:4, 6

God is beauty.
SAINT FRANCIS OF ASSISI

AS YOU PRAISE GOD TODAY

- Give God glory and honor as you worship him in the beauty of his holiness.
- Praise him for making everything beautiful in its time.

GOD IS A SUN

The LORD God is a sun and shield;
the LORD bestows favor and honor;
no good thing does he withhold
from those whose walk is blameless.

PSALM 84:11

God's splendor was like the sunrise;
rays flashed from his hand,
where his power was hidden.

HABAKKUK 3:4

Arise, shine, for your light has come,
and the glory of the LORD rises upon you.
See, darkness covers the earth
and thick darkness is over the peoples,
but the LORD rises upon you
and his glory appears over you.

ISAIAH 60:1–2

AS YOU PRAISE GOD TODAY

- Praise God for the splendor of his glory and light.
- Thank God for the ways in which he has shone the brightness of his glory in your life.

GOD IS YOUR DWELLING PLACE

If you make the Most High your dwelling—
even the LORD, who is my refuge—
then no harm will befall you,
no disaster will come near your tent.
PSALM 91:9–10

LORD, you have been our dwelling place
throughout all generations.
PSALM 90:1

In God we live and move and have our being.
ACTS 17:28

AS YOU PRAISE GOD TODAY

- Remember that your only true dwelling place is in him.
- Praise God for the privilege of having him dwell in you, and also because you can dwell in him forever.
- Think about what it means for you personally to dwell in God.

THE ALMIGHTY

O LORD God Almighty, who is like you?
You are mighty, O LORD, and your faithfulness
surrounds you.
PSALM 89:8

"My name will be great among the nations, from
the rising to the setting of the sun. In every place
incense and pure offerings will be brought to my
name, because my name will be great among the
nations," says the LORD Almighty.
MALACHI 1:11

The twenty-four elders, who were seated on their
thrones before God, fell on their faces and wor-
shiped God, saying:
"We give thanks to you, Lord God Almighty,
the One who is and who was,
because you have taken your great power
and have begun to reign."
REVELATION 11:16–17

AS YOU PRAISE GOD TODAY

- Worship him for being God Almighty, the One
  who was and is and is to come.

GOD IS YOUR FORTRESS

I will say of the LORD, "He is my refuge
and my fortress,
my God, in whom I trust."
PSALM 91:2

He is my loving God and my fortress,
my stronghold and my deliverer,
my shield, in whom I take refuge.
PSALM 144:2

A mighty fortress is our God
A bulwark never failing;
Our helper He amidst the flood
Of mortals ills prevailing.
MARTIN LUTHER

AS YOU PRAISE GOD TODAY

- Remember that as a Christian you stand inside
  the fortress of God. In that fortress, there's no
  reason to ever feel insecure.
- Thank God for being your impenetrable fortress.

GOD IS EVERLASTING

*Stand up and praise the LORD your God, who is
from everlasting to everlasting.
Blessed be your glorious name, and may it be
exalted above all blessing and praise.*

NEHEMIAH 9:5

*Do you not know?
Have you not heard?
The LORD is the everlasting God,
the Creator of the ends of the earth.*

ISAIAH 40:28

There is a hint of the everlasting in the vastness
of the sea.

J. B. PHILLIPS

AS YOU PRAISE GOD TODAY

- Consider the wonder that God is from everlasting
  to everlasting. You are too if you have accepted
  Jesus as your Savior!
- Praise God for being everlasting life itself and for
  allowing us to live in him.

THE LORD IS YOUR MAKER

God created man in his own image,
in the image of God he created him;
male and female he created them.

GENESIS 1:27

We are God's workmanship, created in Christ
Jesus to do good works, which God prepared in
advance for us to do.

EPHESIANS 2:10

In the still air the music lies unheard;
In the rough marble beauty lies unseen;
To make the music and the beauty needs
The master's touch, the sculptor's chisel keen.
Great Master, touch us with Thy skillful hands;
Let not the music that is in us die!
Great Sculptor, hew and polish us; nor let,
Hidden and lost, Thy form within us lie!

MRS. CHARLES E. COWMAN

AS YOU PRAISE GOD TODAY

- Give thanks to God for working in you to make you more like Jesus.
- Ask God to cut away all the blemishes in your character and sculpt you into the image of his Son Jesus.

GOD IS AWESOME

You are awesome, O God, in your sanctuary;
the God of Israel gives power
and strength to his people.
Praise be to God!

PSALM 68:35

Clap your hands, all you nations;
shout to God with cries of joy.
How awesome is the LORD Most High,
the great King over all the earth!

PSALM 47:1–2

Who in the skies above can compare with the LORD?
Who is like the LORD among the heavenly beings?
In the council of the holy ones God is greatly feared;
he is more awesome than all who surround him.

PSALM 89:6–7

AS YOU PRAISE GOD TODAY

- Think about things God has done that show that he is awesome.
- Meditate on his awesomeness and give God glory and honor.

GOD IS YOUR PROVIDER

Jesus said, "Look at the birds of the air; they do not sow or reap or store away in barns, and yet your heavenly Father feeds them. Are you not much more valuable than they?"

MATTHEW 6:26

*"I provide water in the desert
and streams in the wasteland,
to give drink to my people, my chosen,
the people I formed for myself
that they may proclaim my praise," says the LORD.*

ISAIAH 43:20–21

*My God will meet all your needs according to his glorious riches in Christ Jesus.
To our God and Father be glory for ever and ever.
Amen.*

PHILIPPIANS 4:19–20

AS YOU PRAISE GOD TODAY

- Recount the many times God has met your needs and give him glory.
- Thank him that no matter what you will ever need, he will provide for you.

THE RULER OF
THE HEAVENS

Give thanks to the God of heaven.
His love endures forever.
PSALM 136:26

The heavens declare the glory of God;
the skies proclaim the work of his hands.
PSALM 19:1

By the word of the LORD were the heavens made,
their starry host by the breath of his mouth.
PSALM 33:6

He gave a command to the skies above
and opened the doors of the heavens;
he rained down manna for the people to eat,
he gave them the grain of heaven.
PSALM 78:23–24

AS YOU PRAISE GOD TODAY

- Think of all the stars in the sky, and consider that God controls them and knows every minute detail of them.
- Praise him as the God of the Heavens, for his wisdom is beyond our comprehension. A newborn baby seems to us helpless and ignorant, and our most brilliant scientists when they stand before God look much the same way.

GOD IS OMNIPRESENT

Where can I go from your Spirit?
Where can I flee from your presence?
If I go up to the heavens, you are there:
if I make my bed in the depths, you are there.
If I rise on the wings of the dawn,
if I settle on the far side of the sea,
even there your hand will guide me,
your right hand will hold me fast.

PSALM 139:7–10

God is in all things and in every place. There is not a place in the world in which he is not most truly present. Just as birds, wherever they fly, always meet with the air, so we, wherever we go, or wherever we are, always find God present.

SAINT FRANCIS OF SALES

AS YOU PRAISE GOD TODAY

- Think about how awesome it is that God is everywhere all the time and that you are always in his presence.
- Praise God for loving you enough to keep a constant watch over your life.

GOD UPHOLDS YOU

"Do not fear, for I am with you;
do not be dismayed, for I am your God.
I will strengthen you and help you;
I will uphold you with my righteous right hand,"
says the LORD.
ISAIAH 41:10

The LORD upholds all those who fall
and lifts up all who are bowed down.
PSALM 145:14

If the LORD delights in a man's way,
he makes his steps firm;
though he stumble, he will not fall,
for the LORD upholds him with his hand.
PSALM 37:23–24

AS YOU PRAISE GOD TODAY

- Rejoice in the security you experience as you realize God will always uphold you.
- Think of a situation that strikes fear in your heart. Praise God that he is with you and will uphold you with his righteous right hand.

GOD IS PATIENT

The Lord is not slow in keeping his promise, as some understand slowness. He is patient with you, not wanting anyone to perish, but everyone to come to repentance.

2 PETER 3:9

The LORD is slow to anger, abounding in love.

NUMBERS 14:18

"The LORD, the LORD, the compassionate and gracious God, slow to anger, abounding in love and faithfulness, maintaining love to thousands."

EXODUS 34:6

The LORD is gracious and compassionate, slow to anger and rich in love.

PSALM 145:8

AS YOU PRAISE GOD TODAY

- Praise him that although people are often impatient, God is always patient with you.
- Thank God for being slow to anger and giving you the opportunity to make things right with him.

GOD IS YOUR DEFENDER

You hear, O LORD, the desire of the afflicted;
you encourage them, and you listen to their cry,
defending the fatherless and the oppressed,
in order that man, who is of the earth,
may terrify no more.
PSALM 10:17–18

He will defend the afflicted among the people
and save the children of the needy;
he will crush the oppressor.
PSALM 72:4

AS YOU PRAISE GOD TODAY

- Praise God for being your defender whenever you need him to be.
- Thank God that you do not have to defend yourself because he will do it.
- Praise God for defending the fatherless, the widow, the oppressed, and the afflicted.

GOD IS AVAILABLE

God is our refuge and strength,
an ever-present help in trouble.
PSALM 46:1

Jesus said, "Surely I am with you always,
to the very end of the age."
MATTHEW 28:20

Most of us will probably never be invited to the White House to sit down and talk with the President. Most of us can't walk through the door of a state representative without an appointment made months in advance. And most of us wouldn't even be able to drop in unannounced on our pastor and find him in his office, available for a chat. Yet God, the creator of the universe, says that we can come before him at any time, for any reason, and he will not turn us away. He is holy; and he is approachable.

SARAH M. HUPP

AS YOU PRAISE GOD TODAY

- Thank God that although he is pure and holy, he has allowed us to come before his throne in prayer.
- Praise God for never being too busy to listen to you.
- Thank him for being an ever-present help when you are in trouble.

GOD WITH US

IMMANUEL

*The virgin will be with child and will give birth
to a son, and they will call him "Immanuel"—
which means, "God with us."*

MATTHEW 1:23

A little boy said to his mother, "I'm hungry. My
Sunday School teacher talked about God and
chili today. She said Jesus was God *con carne*. Can we
have chili for lunch, please?"

The boy's ears heard "chili," but his teacher was
trying to communicate the miracle of Christ's
humanity. No other religion offers such a gift—God
himself, in the form of Jesus, left heaven to become
flesh and blood, to live on earth. Not con carne, but
incarnate—God with us in the flesh.

SARAH M. HUPP

AS YOU PRAISE GOD TODAY

- Thank him for sending his incarnate Son to live,
  love, and die among us.
- Praise God for sending the Holy Spirit to be
  with us after Jesus left the earth.
- Thank him that the Holy Spirit will live with
  you forever.

MIGHTY ONE

EL-GIBHOR

The Mighty One, God, the LORD,
speaks and summons the earth
from the rising of the sun to the place where it sets.
PSALM 50:1

Mightier than the thunder of the great waters,
mightier than the breakers of the sea—
the LORD on high is mighty.
PSALM 93:4

When the contrary winds of life swirl us in an about-face direction, the Mighty One hovers near and continues to work for our good.

LIFE PROMISES BIBLE

AS YOU PRAISE GOD TODAY

- Give praise that you worship a Mighty God. Those who worship money, or power, or relationships, or anything else eventually find their gods too weak to help them.
- Praise God that he can take your greatest fear and crush it beneath his mighty hand.
- Give him glory for his willingness to use his might on your behalf.

WONDERFUL COUNSELOR

To us a child is born,
to us a son is given,
and the government will be on his shoulders.
And he will be called
Wonderful Counselor, Mighty God,
Everlasting Father, Prince of Peace.

ISAIAH 9:6

"Counselor" points to the Messiah as a king who determines upon and carries out a program of action. As Wonderful Counselor, the coming Son of David will carry out a royal program that will cause all the world to marvel.

REFLECTING GOD STUDY BIBLE

AS YOU PRAISE GOD TODAY

- Praise God for sending Jesus to be your Wonderful Counselor.
- Thank him and Jesus for sending the Holy Spirit to be your Counselor after Jesus ascended to heaven.
- Give God glory for the Counselor, the Spirit of truth, who will teach you all things and remind you of the things Jesus taught.

GOD KEEPS
HIS COVENANT

The LORD your God is God;
he is the faithful God, keeping his covenant
of love to a thousand generations of those
who love him and keep his commands.

DEUTERONOMY 7:9

"Though the mountains be shaken
and the hills be removed,
yet my unfailing love for you will not be shaken
nor my covenant of peace be removed,"
says the LORD, who has compassion on you.

ISAIAH 54:10

He remembers his covenant forever,
the word he commanded,
for a thousand generations.

PSALM 105:8

AS YOU PRAISE GOD TODAY

- Thank God for his covenant of love and peace with you.
- Praise him that he will never break that covenant.

JESUS IS THE PRINCE OF PEACE

Jesus said, "Peace I leave with you;
my peace I give you. I do not give to you as
the world gives. Do not let your hearts be
troubled and do not be afraid."

JOHN 14:27

He was pierced for our transgressions,
he was crushed for our iniquities;
the punishment that brought us peace
was upon him,
and by his wounds we are healed.

ISAIAH 53:5

AS YOU PRAISE GOD TODAY

- Rest in him as the God of peace, and release your cares and concerns to him.
- Cast your cares out of your mind, sit quietly, and feel God's peace enter your heart.
- Thank Jesus for bearing the punishment that bought you peace.

JESUS IS HUMBLE

Jesus said, "Take my yoke upon you and learn from me, for I am gentle and humble in heart, and you will find rest for your souls."
MATTHEW 11:29

Jesus poured water into a basin and began to wash his disciples' feet, drying them with the towel that was wrapped around him.
JOHN 13:5

Being found in appearance as a man,
he humbled himself
and became obedient to death—
even death on a cross!
PHILIPPIANS 2:8

AS YOU PRAISE GOD TODAY

- Praise Jesus for being willing to humble himself and be obedient to death— death on a cross for you.
- Thank Jesus for giving you a wonderful example of what it means to be humble by washing his disciples' feet.
- Worship Jesus for being a Lord who is gentle and humble instead of harsh and arrogant.

THE TRINITY IS UNIFIED

Jesus said, "I and the Father are one."
JOHN 10:30

Although God loves man lavishly, he first bestows his perfect love on his Son, who in turn loves the Father joyously and unceasingly. And though there is no mention of the Father's love for the Holy Spirit, we know that the Trinity was and is ablaze with pure, unadulterated love, because the Spirit's desire is to glorify the Son.

Still more amazing is that the kind of love that exists between the Father and Son can be experienced by you and me. Teaching his hand-picked disciples at the Passover feast, Jesus astounded them with these words, "As the Father has loved me, so have I loved you. Now remain in my love" (John 15:9).

CHARLES STANLEY

AS YOU PRAISE GOD TODAY

- Thank God for the unity shared by him, Jesus, and the Holy Spirit.
- Praise God for the wonder of the three Persons of the Trinity being One.

GOD CARES FOR THE ANIMALS

The high mountains belong to the wild goats;
*   the crags are a refuge for the coneys . . .*
You bring darkness, it becomes night,
*   and all the beasts of the forest prowl.*
*   The lions roar for their prey*
*   and seek their food from God.*
*   The sun rises, and they steal away;*
they return and lie down in their dens . . .
*   How many are your works, O LORD!*
*   In wisdom you made them all;*
*   the earth is full of your creatures.*
*   There is the sea, vast and spacious,*
teeming with creatures beyond number—
*   living things both large and small . . .*
*   These all look to you*
to give them their food at the proper time.
*   When you give it to them,*
*   they gather it up;*
*   when you open your hand,*
*   they are satisfied with good things.*
PSALM 104: 18, 20–22, 24–25, 27–28

AS YOU PRAISE GOD TODAY

- Rejoice as you marvel over all the wonderful creatures God created and takes care of!
- Praise God for opening his hand to all creatures and satisfying them with good things.

GOD IS THE RECONCILER

*God was pleased to have all his fullness dwell
in [Christ], and through him to reconcile to himself all things, whether things on earth or things
in heaven, by making peace through his blood,
shed on the cross.*

COLOSSIANS 1:19–20

*God was reconciling the world to himself
in Christ, not counting men's sins against them.
And he has committed to us the message
of reconciliation.*

2 CORINTHIANS 5:19

Never once is God said to be reconciled to man; it is
always man who is reconciled to God.

WILLIAM BARCLAY

AS YOU PRAISE GOD TODAY

- Praise God for reconciling you to himself.
- Thank him for giving you the opportunity to share
  the message of this reconciliation with others.

THE SPIRIT OF POWER

The Spirit of the LORD will rest on [Jesus]—
the Spirit of wisdom and understanding,
the Spirit of counsel and of power.

ISAIAH 11:2

God did not give us a spirit of timidity, but a
spirit of power, of love and of self-discipline.

2 TIMOTHY 1:7

The basic difference between physical and
spiritual power is that men use physical
power but spiritual power uses men.

JUSTIN WROE NIXON

AS YOU PRAISE GOD TODAY

- Praise God for sending Jesus into the world,
  equipped with the Spirit of power.
- Praise him for the spirit of power he has
  given you.

HE KNOWS WHAT IS IN THE HEART OF MAN

*Jesus did not need man's testimony about man,
for he knew what was in a man.*
JOHN 2:25

*The lamp of the LORD searches the spirit of a man;
it searches out his inmost being.*
PROVERBS 20:27

The LORD knows the thoughts of man.
PSALM 94:11

*Man looks at the outward appearance,
but the LORD looks at the heart.*
1 SAMUEL 16:7

AS YOU PRAISE GOD TODAY

- Praise God for knowing what is in the heart of man.
- Thank him for knowing what is in your heart and revealing it to you.

JESUS IS THE ROOT OF JESSE

A shoot will come up from the stump of Jesse;
from his roots a Branch will bear fruit. . . .
In that day the Root of Jesse will stand as a
banner for the peoples; the nations will rally
to him, and his place of rest will be glorious.
ISAIAH 11:1, 10

One of the elders said to me, "Do not weep! See,
the Lion of the tribe of Judah, the Root of David,
has triumphed. He is able to open the scroll and
its seven seals."
REVELATION 5:5

Jesus said, "I am the Root and the Offspring of
David, and the bright Morning Star."
REVELATION 22:16

AS YOU PRAISE GOD TODAY

- Praise him for his marvelous plan for the
  Messiah to come out of Jesse's lineage.
- Praise God for fulfilling the prophesies of the
  Old Testament by bringing Jesus, the Messiah,
  into the world just as he said he would.

THE GOD OF YOUR SALVATION

EL YESHUATI

"Turn to me and be saved,
all you ends of the earth;
for I am God, and there is no other."
ISAIAH 45:22

Surely God is my salvation;
I will trust and not be afraid.
The LORD, the LORD, is my strength and my song;
he has become my salvation.
ISAIAH 12:2

My soul finds rest in God alone;
my salvation comes from him.
PSALM 62:1

Everyone who calls
on the name of the Lord will be saved.
ACTS 2:21

AS YOU PRAISE GOD TODAY

- Praise him for his wonderful gift of salvation.
- Thank God for saving everyone who calls on his name.

THE UPRIGHT ONE

The path of the righteous is level;
O upright One, you make the way
of the righteous smooth.

ISAIAH 26:7

Good and upright is the LORD;
therefore he instructs sinners in his ways.

PSALM 25:8

The righteous will still bear fruit in old age,
they will stay fresh and green,
proclaiming, "The LORD is upright;
he is my Rock, and there is no wickedness in him."

PSALM 92:14–15

AS YOU PRAISE GOD TODAY

- Praise him for being faithful, consistent, and pure.
- Thank God for being totally upright and trustworthy.
- Reflect on this attribute of his and how it affects your life.

GOD IS A REVEALER

*"No eye has seen,
no ear has heard,
no mind has conceived
what God has prepared for those who love him"—
but God has revealed it to us by his Spirit.
The Spirit searches all things, even the deep
things of God.*
1 CORINTHIANS 2:9–10

*"Call to me and I will answer you and tell you
great and unsearchable things you do not know."*
JEREMIAH 33:3

*Jesus said, "When he, the Spirit of truth, comes,
he will guide you into all truth. He will not
speak on his own; he will speak only what he
hears, and he will tell you what is yet to come."*
JOHN 16:13

AS YOU PRAISE GOD TODAY

- Praise God for sending the Spirit to reveal the things he has prepared for you.
- Thank God for his prophets who shared God's dreams and visions in his Word.

GOD SHOWS HIMSELF TO MAN

*"I will show my greatness and my holiness, and
I will make myself known in the sight of many
nations. Then they will know that I am the LORD."*

EZEKIEL 38:23

*"I will show love to the house of Judah; and I will
save them—not by bow, sword or battle, or by
horses and horsemen, but by the LORD their God."*

HOSEA 1:7

*"On my servants, both men and women,
I will pour out my Spirit in those days.
I will show wonders in the heavens
and on the earth,
blood and fire and billows of smoke."*

JOEL 2:29–30

AS YOU PRAISE GOD TODAY

- Thank him for sharing his holiness and greatness with you.
- Praise God for showing you various attributes of
  his character.
- Praise God for the wonders he shows in the
  heavens and on the earth.

GOD IS FULL OF KNOWLEDGE

The LORD gives wisdom,
and from his mouth come knowledge
and understanding.
PROVERBS 2:6

By his knowledge the deeps were divided,
and the clouds let drop the dew.
PROVERBS 3:20

To the man who pleases him, God gives wisdom,
knowledge and happiness.
ECCLESIASTES 2:26

The earth will be full of the knowledge of the LORD
as the waters cover the sea.
ISAIAH 11:9

AS YOU PRAISE GOD TODAY

- Give God glory for the wealth of his knowledge which was powerful enough to divide the deeps.
- Thank him for watching over knowledge.
- Praise God for giving his knowledge to you.
- Rejoice that one day the earth will be filled with the knowledge of the Lord as the waters cover the sea.

JESUS IS YOUR REDEEMER

Christ redeemed us from the curse of the law by becoming a curse for us, for it is written: "Cursed is everyone who is hung on a tree." He redeemed us in order that the blessing given to Abraham might come to the Gentiles through Christ Jesus.

GALATIANS 3:13–14

We wait for the blessed hope—the glorious appearing of our great God and Savior, Jesus Christ, who gave himself for us to redeem us from all wickedness and to purify for himself a people that are his very own, eager to do what is good.

TITUS 2:13–14

Once I was a slave to sin. I sold myself out for nothing, but all the money in the world could not buy my freedom. So You bought me back with Your own life and set me free. Sin made me worthless, but to You I am priceless. I praise You my Redeemer.

NIV WORSHIP BIBLE

AS YOU PRAISE GOD TODAY

- Praise Jesus for becoming a curse for you that the blessing given to Abraham might be yours.
- Praise God for redeeming you from all wickedness, so you could become his own.

GOD BESTOWS FAVOR

*"In the time of my favor I will answer you,
and in the day of salvation I will help you,"
says the LORD.*

ISAIAH 49:8

*Surely, O LORD, you bless the righteous;
you surround them with your favor as with a shield.*

PSALM 5:12

*The LORD's anger lasts only a moment,
but his favor lasts a lifetime.*

PSALM 30:5

AS YOU PRAISE GOD TODAY

- Praise him for surrounding you with favor.
- Thank God for his favor lasts a lifetime.
- Praise Jesus for proclaiming the year of the Lord's favor.

GOD IS A FINISHER

*He who began a good work in you will carry it
on to completion until the day of Christ Jesus.*
PHILIPPIANS 1:6

*The LORD will fulfill his purpose for me;
your love, O LORD, endures forever—
do not abandon the works of your hands.*
PSALM 138:8

*He will keep you strong to the end, so that you will
be blameless on the day of our Lord Jesus Christ.*
1 CORINTHIANS 1:8

*When he had received the drink, Jesus said,
"It is finished." With that, he bowed his head
and gave up his spirit.*
JOHN 19:30

AS YOU PRAISE GOD TODAY

- Thank God for the good work he has begun in
  you, and thank him that he will finish it.
- Praise Jesus for seeing his assignment through to
  the end and finishing it.

JESUS

Y'SHUA

An angel of the Lord said to Joseph, "You are to give him the name Jesus, because he will save his people from their sins."

MATTHEW 1:21

God exalted him to the highest place and gave him the name that is above every name, that at the name of Jesus every knee should bow, in heaven and on earth and under the earth, and every tongue confess that Jesus Christ is Lord, to the glory of God the Father.

PHILIPPIANS 2:9–11

AS YOU PRAISE GOD TODAY

- Give Jesus glory because his name is above all names.
- Reflect on the name of Jesus and the power behind it.
- Thank Jesus that his very name tells you that he will save you from your sin.

I AM HE

"Even to your old age and gray hairs
I am he, I am he who will sustain you.
I have made you and I will carry you;
I will sustain you and I will rescue you."

ISAIAH 46:4

Jesus said, "I am telling you now before it
happens, so that when it does happen you will
believe that I am He."

JOHN 13:19

"I, even I, am he who comforts you."

ISAIAH 51:12

AS YOU PRAISE GOD TODAY

- Allow him to give you the peace and assurance
  that "He is who he says he is."
- Be still and know that he is God.

GOD IS THE CREATOR OF ISRAEL

"I am the LORD, your Holy One,
Israel's Creator, your King."
ISAIAH 43:15

God said, "Your name will be Abraham, for I
have made you a father of many nations. I
will make you very fruitful; I will make
nations of you, and kings will come from you.
I will establish my covenant as an everlasting
covenant between me and you and your
descendants after you for the generations to
come, to be your God and the God of your
descendants after you. The whole land of
Canaan, where you are now an alien, I will
give as an everlasting possession to you and your
descendants after you; and I will be their God."
GENESIS 17:5–8

AS YOU PRAISE GOD TODAY

- Praise God for his faithfulness in creating the nation of Israel.
- Give him glory as the Creator of Israel and its King.

GOD IS HOLY

Just as he who called you is holy,
so be holy in all you do.
1 PETER 1:15

I saw the LORD seated on a throne, high and
exalted, and the train of his robe filled the tem-
ple. Above him were seraphs, each with six wings:
. . . And they were calling to one another:
"Holy, holy, holy is the LORD Almighty;
the whole earth is full of his glory."
ISAIAH 6:1–3

Each of the four living creatures had six wings
and was covered with eyes all around, even under
his wings. Day and night they never stop saying:
"Holy, holy, holy
is the Lord God Almighty,
who was, and is, and is to come."
REVELATION 4:8

AS YOU PRAISE GOD TODAY

- Worship him as in these verses, saying, "Holy holy, holy is the Lord God Almighty."
- Praise God for being holy and for cleansing you, so you can be holy, too.

GOD IS THE FIRST
AND THE LAST

*"Listen to me, O Jacob,
Israel, whom I have called:
I am he;
I am the first and I am the last.
My own hand laid the foundations of the earth,
and my right hand spread out the heavens;
when I summon them,
they all stand up together."*

ISAIAH 48:12–13

*"Do not be afraid. I am the First and the Last,"
says the Lord.*

REVELATION 1:17

*"This is what the LORD says—
Israel's King and Redeemer, the LORD Almighty:
I am the first and I am the last;
apart from me there is no God."*

ISAIAH 44:6

AS YOU PRAISE GOD TODAY

- Reflect on why it is so important that God is the first and last and what this means to you.
- Praise God for being the first and the last, and that apart from him there is no other God.

JESUS IS THE GATE

Jesus said, "I tell you the truth, I am the gate for the sheep. . . . I am the gate; whoever enters through me will be saved. He will come in and go out, and find pasture."

JOHN 10:7–9

Jesus said, "Enter through the narrow gate. For wide is the gate and broad is the road that leads to destruction, and many enter through it. But small is the gate and narrow the road that leads to life, and only a few find it."

MATTHEW 7:13–14

You are the gate that leads to the fold of salvation. You are the fold in which I find safety. When I am in danger, You lay down Your own life for me. You give me the gift of life, life to the full. Oh to know You, gracious Shepherd, and to be known by You—this is true life!

NIV WORSHIP BIBLE

AS YOU PRAISE GOD TODAY

- Thank Jesus for being the gate through which you can enter to be saved.
- Reflect on what it means to be one of his sheep, passing through the gate to find pasture.

THE GOD OF MIRACLES

I will remember the deeds of the LORD;
yes, I will remember your miracles of long ago.
PSALM 77:11

You are the God who performs miracles;
you display your power among the peoples.
PSALM 77:14

Glory in his holy name;
let the hearts of those who seek the LORD rejoice.
Look to the LORD and his strength;
seek his face always.
Remember the wonders he has done,
his miracles, and the judgments he pronounced.
PSALM 105:3–5

AS YOU PRAISE GOD TODAY

- Rejoice that he is a God who does miracles!
- As in the first verse above, remember the miraculous things God has done and praise him for them.

JESUS IS THE LIBERATOR

Jesus said,
"The Spirit of the Lord is on me,
because he has anointed me
to preach good news to the poor.
He has sent me to proclaim freedom for the prisoners
and recovery of sight for the blind,
to release the oppressed, to proclaim the year of
the Lord's favor."

LUKE 4:18–19

The Lord is the Spirit, and where the Spirit
of the Lord is, there is freedom.

2 CORINTHIANS 3:17

It is for freedom that Christ has set us free. Stand
firm, then, and do not let yourselves be burdened
again by a yoke of slavery.

GALATIANS 5:1

AS YOU PRAISE GOD TODAY

- Praise him for setting you free.
- Thank God for the many ways he has set you and all who accept him, free.

GOD HAS A MIGHTY, OUTSTRETCHED ARM

"With my great power and outstretched arm I made the earth and its people and the animals that are on it, and I give it to anyone I please."
JEREMIAH 27:5

Ah, Sovereign LORD, you have made the heavens and the earth by your great power and outstretched arm. Nothing is too hard for you.
JEREMIAH 32:17

*Sing to the LORD a new song,
for he has done marvelous things;
his right hand and his holy arm
have worked salvation for him.*
PSALM 98:1

AS YOU PRAISE GOD TODAY

- Praise him that his outstretched arm reaches down into every detail of your life, and he wants you to let him hold you in his mighty hand.
- Praise God that nothing is too hard for him.
- Ask God to help you rely on the strength of his arm and not on your own power.

JESUS IS THE MAN OF SORROWS

He was despised and rejected by men,
a man of sorrows, and familiar with suffering.
Like one from whom men hide their faces
he was despised, and we esteemed him not.

ISAIAH 53:3

We do not have a high priest who is unable to
sympathize with our weaknesses, but we have one
who has been tempted in every way, just as we
are—yet was without sin.

HEBREWS 4:15

AS YOU PRAISE GOD TODAY

- Consider that no matter how much you've suffered, Christ suffered far more—and he didn't have to suffer at all. He chose to suffer for your sake.

- Be thankful that your God knows exactly what it is to be a human being.

- Take heart if you've ever been despised or rejected. You stand in great company.

JESUS IS THE RIGHTEOUS SERVANT

Jesus said, "Whoever wants to become great among you must be your servant, and whoever wants to be first must be your slave—just as the Son of Man did not come to be served, but to serve, and to give his life as a ransom for many."

MATTHEW 20:26–28

"Here is my servant, whom I uphold, my chosen one in whom I delight; I will put my Spirit on him and he will bring justice to the nations."

ISAIAH 42:1

AS YOU PRAISE GOD TODAY

- Thank him for his amazing desire to serve instead of being served when he came to Earth.
- Think about what kind of servant Jesus was and what he did as a servant.
- Ask Jesus to make you a servant like he was.

GOD IS LIKE A HUSBAND

Your Maker is your husband—
the LORD Almighty is his name—
the Holy One of Israel is your Redeemer;
he is called the God of all the earth.

ISAIAH 54:5

Husbands, love your wives, just as Christ loved
the church and gave himself up for her to make
her holy, cleansing her by the washing with water
through the word, and to present her to himself as
a radiant church, without stain or wrinkle or
any other blemish, but holy and blameless.

EPHESIANS 5:25–27

AS YOU PRAISE GOD TODAY

- Reflect on how God has been like a husband in your life.
- Praise Jesus for the wonderful way he has shown his love for his bride, the Church.

GOD IS A RESTORER

*The God of all grace, who called you to his
eternal glory in Christ, after you have suffered
a little while, will himself restore you and make
you strong, firm and steadfast.*

1 PETER 5:10

*"I will not accuse forever,
nor will I always be angry,
for then the spirit of man would grow
faint before me—
the breath of man that I have created. . . .
I have seen his ways, but I will heal him;
I will guide him and restore comfort to him,
creating praise on the lips of
the mourners in Israel."*

ISAIAH 57:16, 18–19

AS YOU PRAISE GOD TODAY

- Praise him that he can restore you or anyone or
  anything else that has been broken or devastated.
  Praise him for wanting to make you whole.
- Ask God to pick up the pieces of your broken-
  ness and put you back together. He can and will
  restore you.

JESUS IS THE ASCENDED LORD

*Jesus was taken up before the apostles' very eyes,
and a cloud hid him from their sight.*

ACTS 1:9

When Christ returned to heaven, he withdrew his physical presence from our sight. He didn't stop being with the disciples but by the ascension fulfilled his promise to be with us to the end of the world. As his body was raised to heaven, so his power and reign have spread to the uttermost parts.

JOHN CALVIN

AS YOU PRAISE GOD TODAY

- Rejoice that Jesus ascended to the right hand of the Father and now fills the whole universe.
- Praise God for making Jesus' enemies a footstool for Jesus' feet when he ascended to his Father's right hand.
- Rejoice that Jesus led his enemies captive when he ascended on high.

GOD IS LIKE A POTTER

O LORD, you are our Father.
We are the clay, you are the potter;
we are all the work of your hand.

ISAIAH 64:8

If man would but believe they are in the process of creation, and consent to be made—let the Maker handle them as the potter the clay, yielding themselves in resplendent motion and submissive, hopeful action with the turning of His wheel—they would soon find themselves able to welcome every pressure of that hand on them, even when it was felt in pain; and sometimes not only to believe but to recognize the divine end in view, the bringing of a son unto glory.

MRS. CHARLES E. COWMAN

AS YOU PRAISE GOD TODAY

- Rejoice that he is making you into a wonderful creation; bringing great glory to him.
- Praise God that he has a design for your life, even if you don't yet know what it is.

GOD IS YOUR COMFORTER

The ransomed of the LORD will return.
They will enter Zion with singing;
everlasting joy will crown their heads.
Gladness and joy will overtake them,
and sorrow and sighing will flee away.
"I, even I, am he who comforts you," says the LORD.
ISAIAH 51:11–12

For the LORD comforts his people
and will have compassion on his afflicted ones.
ISAIAH 49:13

Praise be to the God and Father of our Lord Jesus
Christ, the Father of compassion and the God of
all comfort, who comforts us in all our troubles,
so that we can comfort those in any trouble with
the comfort we ourselves have received from God.
2 CORINTHIANS 1:3–4

AS YOU PRAISE GOD TODAY

- Think of all the times and ways God has comforted you.
- Praise him for being the One to whom you can turn with all your fears and sorrows.

THE LIVING GOD

ELOHIM CHAIYIM

The LORD is the true God;
he is the living God, the eternal King.
JEREMIAH 10:10

How lovely is your dwelling place,
O LORD Almighty!
My soul yearns, even faints,
for the courts of the LORD;
my heart and my flesh cry out
for the living God.
PSALM 84:1–2

We are the temple of the living God.
As God has said: "I will live with them
and walk among them, and I will be their God,
and they will be my people."
2 CORINTHIANS 6:16

AS YOU PRAISE GOD TODAY

- Praise him for not being just a theological proposition, but a living, active Being who loves you and wants to be the center of your life.
- Reflect on the ways you have witnessed God as the living God in your life, and thank him for the opportunities.

GOD IS NEAR

ELOHAY MIKAROV

*The LORD is near to all who call on him,
to all who call on him in truth.*
PSALM 145:18

*Now in Christ Jesus you who once were far away have
been brought near through the blood of Christ.*
EPHESIANS 2:13

*From one man he made every nation of men,
that they should inhabit the whole earth;
and he determined the times set for them and the
exact places where they should live. God did this
so that men would seek him and perhaps reach
out for him and find him, though he is not far
from each one of us.*
ACTS 17:26–27

AS YOU PRAISE GOD TODAY

- Praise him for always being near, even when he seems to be far away.
- Think of all the times you have felt or seen God's presence in your life. Thank him for those times.

JESUS IS THE LORD YOUR RIGHTEOUSNESS

God made him who had no sin to be sin for us,
so that in him we might become
the righteousness of God.
2 CORINTHIANS 5:21

Christ died for sins once for all, the righteous for
the unrighteous, to bring you to God.
1 PETER 3:18

He himself bore our sins in his body on the tree,
so that we might die to sins and live for
righteousness.
1 PETER 2:24

"He committed no sin,
and no deceit was found in his mouth."
1 PETER 2:22

AS YOU PRAISE GOD TODAY

- Praise him that you stand righteous before him, not because of what you've done, but because of the sacrifice of Jesus.
- Thank Jesus for his willingness to become sin, so you could become the righteousness of God in him.

THE GOD OF ALL MANKIND

ELOHAY KOL BASAR

What is man that you are mindful of him,
the son of man that you care for him?
You made him a little lower than
the heavenly beings
and crowned him with glory and honor.

PSALM 8:4–5

Every soul belongs to God and exists by his
pleasure. God being who and what he is, and
we being who and what we are, the only thinkable
relation between us is one of full lordship on his part
and complete submission on ours. We owe him
every honor that it is in our power to give him.

A. W. TOZER

AS YOU PRAISE GOD TODAY

- Reflect on the awesomeness of his creation of
  man, and praise him as you consider that he is
  God of all mankind.
- Praise him that although he is God of all, he is
  mindful of you.

THE LORD WHO MAKES HOLY

JEHOVAH M'KADESH

We have been made holy through the sacrifice of the body of Jesus Christ once for all.
HEBREWS 10:10

Holiness is not the laborious acquisition of virtue from without, but the expression of the Christ-life from within.

JOHN WILLIAM CHARLES WAND

AS YOU PRAISE GOD TODAY

- Rejoice in the fact that you don't have to make yourself holy, but through the sacrifice and blood of Jesus Christ, you have been made holy once and for all.
- As one of his family members, join Jesus as he sings God's praises in the presence of the congregation.

JESUS IS AN INTERCESSOR

*We do not know what we ought to pray for,
but the Spirit himself intercedes for us with
groans that words cannot express. And he who
searches our hearts knows the mind of the Spirit,
because the Spirit intercedes for the saints
in accordance with God's will.*

ROMANS 8:26–27

*Christ Jesus, who died—more than that, who
was raised to life—is at the right hand of God
and is also interceding for us.*

ROMANS 8:34

AS YOU PRAISE GOD TODAY

- Rejoice as you reflect on Jesus and the Holy Spirit interceding for you.
- When you don't know what to pray, the Spirit intercedes for you in accordance with God's will. Thank him for this incredible gift.

GOD IS YOUR PROTECTOR

*The LORD loves the just
and will not forsake his faithful ones.
They will be protected forever.*

PSALM 37:28

*If you make the Most High your dwelling—
even the LORD, who is my refuge—
then no harm will befall you,
no disaster will come near your tent.
For he will command his angels concerning you
to guard you in all your ways.*

PSALM 91:9–11

*The Lord is faithful, and he will strengthen
and protect you from the evil one.*

2 THESSALONIANS 3:3

AS YOU PRAISE GOD TODAY

- Thank him for his hand of protection.
- Praise God for giving his angels charge over you to guard you in all your ways.

GOD IS THE ANCIENT OF DAYS

As I looked,
thrones were set in place,
and the Ancient of Days took his seat.
His clothing was as white as snow;
the hair of his head was white like wool.
His throne was flaming with fire,
and its wheels were all ablaze.

DANIEL 7:9

In my vision at night I looked, and there before me
was one like a son of man, coming with the clouds
of heaven. He approached the Ancient of Days and
was led into his presence. He was given authority,
glory and sovereign power; all peoples, nations and
men of every language worshiped him.

DANIEL 7:13–14

AS YOU PRAISE GOD TODAY

- Consider that he is the same today as he was during the times of Jesus, Moses, Abraham, and all the way back to Adam.
- Worship God as you reflect on the description of the majestic Ancient of Days in Daniel 7:9.
- Praise God for giving the Son of Man authority, glory, and sovereign power.

GOD IS A RULER OF RULERS

The king's heart is in the hand of the LORD;
he directs it like a watercourse
wherever he pleases.

PROVERBS 21:1

We observe the world's leaders and assume that, for better or worse, they are in control. We at times presume that they hold the power of life and death and have the ability to change the course of history. But, in reality, God both establishes rulers and deposes them. Although we often fail to understand why he allows certain events to occur, we live in the comfort of knowing that nothing happens without his permission.

LIFE PROMISES BIBLE

AS YOU PRAISE GOD TODAY

- Praise him that even earthly governments rule only with his permission, and only he has the power to make them stand or fall.
- Praise Jesus as the head over every power and authority.

JESUS IS THE ANOINTED ONE

The Spirit of the Sovereign LORD is on me,
because the LORD has anointed me
to preach good news to the poor.
He has sent me to bind up the brokenhearted,
to proclaim freedom for the captives
and release from darkness for the prisoners,
to proclaim the year of the LORD's favor
and the day of vengeance of our God,
to comfort all who mourn,
and provide for those who grieve in Zion—
to bestow on them a crown of beauty
instead of ashes,
the oil of gladness
instead of mourning,
and a garment of praise
instead of a spirit of despair.

ISAIAH 61:1–3

AS YOU PRAISE GOD TODAY

- Praise him for anointing Jesus to bring us the Good News of salvation, healing for broken hearts, freedom, comfort, beauty, gladness, and praise.
- Praise God for anointing Jesus to heal all who were under the power of the devil.

JESUS IS LORD
OF ALL THE EARTH

The earth is the LORD's, and everything in it,
the world, and all who live in it;
for he founded it upon the seas
and established it upon the waters.

PSALM 24:1–2

The LORD reigns, let the earth be glad;
let the distant shores rejoice.
Clouds and thick darkness surround him;
righteousness and justice are the foundation
of his throne.
Fire goes before him
and consumes his foes on every side.
His lightning lights up the world;
the earth sees and trembles.
The mountains melt like wax before the LORD,
before the LORD of all the earth.

PSALM 97:1–5

AS YOU PRAISE GOD TODAY

- Spend some time reflecting on the various aspects of nature—clouds, wind, rain, trees, mountains, oceans and rivers, lightning. Rejoice as you consider that even the wind and the waves obeyed Jesus.

GOD IS ABLE

"I am the LORD, the God of all mankind.
Is anything too hard for me?"
JEREMIAH 32:27

"With God all things are possible."
MATTHEW 19:26

The angel told Mary, "Even Elizabeth your
relative is going to have a child in her old age,
and she who was said to be barren is in her sixth
month. For nothing is impossible with God."
LUKE 1:36–37

God raised Jesus from the dead, freeing him from
the agony of death, because it was impossible
for death to keep its hold on him.
ACTS 2:24

AS YOU PRAISE GOD TODAY

- Honor him for being such an awesome God for whom nothing is too difficult.
- Reflect on the "impossible" things God has done for you and thank him.

THE EXALTED GOD

ELOHAY MAROM

Great is the LORD in Zion;
he is exalted over all the nations.
PSALM 99:2

The LORD is exalted, for he dwells on high;
he will fill Zion with justice and righteousness.
ISAIAH 33:5

Let them praise the name of the LORD,
for his name alone is exalted;
his splendor is above the earth and the heavens.
PSALM 148:13

I saw the LORD seated on a throne, high and
exalted, and the train of his robe filled the temple.
ISAIAH 6:1

AS YOU PRAISE GOD TODAY

- Reflect on the amazing verses above. What do they tell you about God?
- Praise him that he has revealed his majesty to us!
- Worship him as the exalted God, exalted over all.

JESUS HAS AUTHORITY

Jesus came to the eleven disciples and said, "All authority in heaven and on earth has been given to me. Therefore go and make disciples of all nations, baptizing them in the name of the Father and of the Son and of the Holy Spirit, and teaching them to obey everything I have commanded you."

MATTHEW 28:18–20

The people were amazed at Jesus' teaching, because he taught them as one who had authority, not as the teachers of the law.

MARK 1:22

AS YOU PRAISE GOD TODAY

- Praise him for giving Jesus authority to heal and forgive sins.
- Reflect on Mark 1:22. Give Jesus praise as you consider how he taught with such authority that it amazed the people.

JESUS IS YOUR MASTER

*A squall came down on the lake, so that the boat
was being swamped, and [the disciples and Jesus]
were in great danger.
The disciples went and woke Jesus, saying,
"Master, Master, we're going to drown!"
He got up and rebuked the wind and the raging
waters; the storm subsided, and all was calm. . . .
In fear and amazement they asked one another,
"Who is this? He commands even the winds and
the water, and they obey him."*

LUKE 8:23–25

AS YOU PRAISE GOD TODAY

- Praise Jesus for being a kindly, compassionate,
  and understanding master.
- Give him glory and honor as your Master.

GOD IS A REFINER

Praise our God, O peoples,
let the sound of his praise be heard;
he has preserved our lives
and kept our feet from slipping.
For you, O God, tested us;
you refined us like silver.

PSALM 66:8–10

We wait for the blessed hope—the glorious
appearing of our great God and Savior, Jesus
Christ, who gave himself for us to redeem us from
all wickedness and to purify for himself a people
that are his very own, eager to do what is good.

TITUS 2:13–14

AS YOU PRAISE GOD TODAY

- Praise him for refining and purifying you. Praise God for the pure gold and silver he is making of your life.
- Let the sound of your praise be heard as in Psalm 66:8–10.
- Thank Jesus for giving himself to purify you.

THE LORD IS YOUR RESCUER

The LORD reached down from on high
and took hold of me;
he drew me out of deep waters.
He rescued me from my powerful enemy,
from my foes, who were too strong for me. . . .
He brought me out into a spacious place;
he rescued me because he delighted in me.

PSALM 18:16–17, 19

"As a shepherd looks after his scattered flock
when he is with them, so will I look after
my sheep. I will rescue them from all the places
where they were scattered on a day of clouds
and darkness," says the LORD.

EZEKIEL 34:12

AS YOU PRAISE GOD TODAY

- Praise him for rescuing you even to your old age.
- Praise God that no matter how strong your enemy is, God will rescue you because he delights in you.

GOD RENEWS YOU

Those who hope in the LORD
will renew their strength.
They will soar on wings like eagles;
they will run and not grow weary,
they will walk and not be faint.
ISAIAH 40:31

God saved us through the washing of rebirth and
renewal by the Holy Spirit, whom he poured out
on us generously through Jesus Christ our Savior.
TITUS 3:5–6

AS YOU PRAISE GOD TODAY

- Praise God that as you hope in him, he will renew your strength.
- Rejoice that you are saved through the washing of rebirth and the renewal of the Holy Spirit.

CHRIST (MESSIAH)

*"What about you?" Jesus asked. "Who do you say
that I am?"*
*Simon Peter answered, "You are the Christ, the
Son of the living God."*
*Jesus replied, "Blessed are you, Simon son of
Jonah, for this was not revealed to you by man,
but by my Father in heaven."*
MATTHEW 16:15–17

*The high priest asked Jesus, "Are you the Christ,
the Son of the Blessed One?"*
*"I am," said Jesus. "And you will see the Son of
Man sitting at the right hand of the Mighty One
and coming on the clouds of heaven."*
MARK 14:61–62

AS YOU PRAISE GOD TODAY

- Praise him for the free gift of salvation through
  Christ.
- Thank God for revealing to you that Jesus is the
  Christ!

JESUS IS THE SON OF DAVID

In love a throne will be established;
in faithfulness a man will sit on it—
one from the house of David—
one who in judging seeks justice
and speeds the cause of righteousness.
ISAIAH 16:5

Two blind men followed [Jesus], calling out,
"Have mercy on us, Son of David!"
. . . Jesus touched [the eyes of the two blind men]
and said, "According to your faith will it be
done to you"; and their sight was restored.
MATTHEW 9:27, 29–30

AS YOU PRAISE GOD TODAY

- Praise him for promising that the Messiah would come through the line of David and for keeping his promise.

JESUS IS YOUR EXAMPLE

Jesus said to his disciples, "Now that I,
your Lord and Teacher, have washed your feet,
you also should wash one another's feet.
I have set you an example that you should do
as I have done for you."
JOHN 13:14–15

Your attitude should be the same
as that of Christ Jesus:
Who, being in very nature God,
did not consider equality with God
something to be grasped,
but made himself nothing,
taking the very nature of a servant,
being made in human likeness.
PHILIPPIANS 2:5–7

AS YOU PRAISE GOD TODAY

- Praise Jesus for setting the ultimate example for you as you live your life in Christ.
- Give Jesus glory not only for setting the example, but also for doing it without any sin whatsoever.

GOD FILLS YOUR MOUTH

Jesus said to his disciples, "When they arrest you, do not worry about what to say or how to say it. At that time you will be given what to say, for it will not be you speaking, but the Spirit of your Father speaking through you."

MATTHEW 10:19–20

Jesus said to his disciples, "Make up your mind not to worry beforehand how you will defend yourselves. For I will give you words and wisdom that none of your adversaries will be able to resist or contradict."

LUKE 21:14–15

"I am the LORD your God, who brought you up out of Egypt. Open wide your mouth, and I will fill it."

PSALM 81:10

AS YOU PRAISE GOD TODAY

- Praise him for giving you the right words to say just when you need them.

GOD IS A JUDGE

SHAPHAT

God is a righteous judge.
PSALM 7:11

Paul says that we must all, preachers and other people alike, "appear before the judgment seat of Christ" [2 Corinthians 5:10]. But if you will learn here and now how to live under the scrutiny of Christ's pure light, your final judgment will bring you only delight in seeing the work God has done in you. Live constantly reminding yourself of the judgment seat of Christ, and walk in the knowledge of the holiness He has given you.

OSWALD CHAMBERS

AS YOU PRAISE GOD TODAY

- Praise him for being a righteous judge.
- Thank him for giving you the chance to repent when you need to, so God can judge you not guilty and forgive you.

THE HOLY SPIRIT IS LIKE A DOVE

As soon as Jesus was baptized, he went up out of the water. At that moment heaven was opened, and he saw the Spirit of God descending like a dove and lighting on him.

MATTHEW 3:16

In the same way, the Spirit helps us in our weakness. We do not know what we ought to pray for, but the Spirit himself intercedes for us with groans that words cannot express. And he who searches our hearts knows the mind of the Spirit, because the Spirit intercedes for the saints in accordance with God's will.

ROMANS 8:26–27

Jesus has gone to prepare a place for us, and the Holy Spirit has been sent to prepare us for that place.

AUTHOR UNKNOWN

AS YOU PRAISE GOD TODAY

- Thank him for using the symbol of a gentle dove to represent the Holy Spirit and his work in your life.

JESUS IS THE BELOVED SON

A voice from heaven said, "This is my Son, whom I love; with him I am well pleased."

MATTHEW 3:17

A father giving away a beloved son is beyond our understanding. Yet that is precisely what God did for us. We were full of sin and shame. Nothing we did could change it. Motivated by his love for us, God gave away his one and only Son to set us free from the bondage of our shame.

CHRISTIAN GROWTH STUDY BIBLE

AS YOU PRAISE GOD TODAY

- Thank God for the wonderful example he and Jesus have set of a loving parent/child relationship.
- Praise him for the great love and honor he has bestowed upon his Son.
- Thank him for sacrificing his beloved Son for you.

THE HOLY SPIRIT DWELLS WITHIN YOU

Jesus said, "I will ask the Father, and he will give you another Counselor to be with you forever— the Spirit of truth. The world cannot accept him, because it neither sees him nor knows him. But you know him, for he lives with you and will be in you."

JOHN 14:16–17

Don't you know that you yourselves are God's temple and that God's Spirit lives in you?

1 CORINTHIANS 3:16

In Christ you too are being built together to become a dwelling in which God lives by his Spirit.

EPHESIANS 2:22

AS YOU PRAISE GOD TODAY

- Thank him for sending the Holy Spirit to dwell within you.
- Praise God for the comfort, strength, and guidance you receive from his Spirit.

GOD IS ALL-KNOWING

*Great is our LORD and mighty in power;
his understanding has no limit.*
PSALM 147:5

*Nothing in all creation is hidden from
God's sight. Everything is uncovered
and laid bare before the eyes of him
to whom we must give account.*
HEBREWS 4:13

*God is greater than our hearts,
and he knows everything.*
1 JOHN 3:20

AS YOU PRAISE GOD TODAY

- Rejoice in the fact that God knows everything.
- Thank him for knowing and providing for your
  every need even before you speak it.

JESUS IS THE SON OF THE FATHER

Jesus said, "All things have been committed to me by my Father. No one knows the Son except the Father, and no one knows the Father except the Son and those to whom the Son chooses to reveal him."

MATTHEW 11:27

Jesus said, "I tell you the truth, the Son can do nothing by himself; he can do only what he sees his Father doing, because whatever the Father does the Son also does."

JOHN 5:19

Jesus received honor and glory from God the Father when the voice came to him from the Majestic Glory, saying, "This is my Son, whom I love; with him I am well pleased."

2 PETER 1:17

AS YOU PRAISE GOD TODAY

- Praise him that you can know the Father through Jesus the Son.
- The Father and the Son give honor to one another. Thank God for the privilege of joining with them in giving honor to them.

GOD HAS MADE YOU AN HEIR

If you belong to Christ, then you are Abraham's seed, and heirs according to the promise.
GALATIANS 3:29

You are no longer a slave, but a son; and since you are a son, God has made you also an heir.
GALATIANS 4:7

You also were included in Christ when you heard the word of truth, the gospel of your salvation. Having believed, you were marked in him with a seal, the promised Holy Spirit, who is a deposit guaranteeing our inheritance until the redemption of those who are God's possession— to the praise of his glory.
EPHESIANS 1:13–14

AS YOU PRAISE GOD TODAY

- Rejoice in the fact that you are no longer a slave, but a child of God and also an heir.
- Thank him for sending the Holy Spirit who is your deposit guaranteeing your inheritance.

GOD COMMANDS ANGELS

The LORD will command his angels
concerning you
to guard you in all your ways;
they will lift you up in their hands,
so that you will not strike your foot against
a stone.

PSALM 91:11–12

Praise the LORD, you his angels,
you mighty ones who do his bidding,
who obey his word.

PSALM 103:20

Jesus said, "Do you think I cannot call on my
Father, and he will at once put at my disposal
more than twelve legions of angels?"

MATTHEW 26:53

AS YOU PRAISE GOD TODAY

- Marvel as you consider that Jesus will send out his angels at the end of the world to rout out all sin and evil.
- Praise him that one day he will come with his angels to take his children home to heaven!

GOD IS A REWARDER

"I, the LORD, love justice;
I hate robbery and iniquity.
In my faithfulness I will reward [my people]
and make an everlasting covenant with them."

ISAIAH 61:8

Without faith it is impossible to please God,
because anyone who comes to him must believe
that he exists and that he rewards those who
earnestly seek him.

HEBREWS 11:6

The LORD has dealt with me according
to my righteousness;
according to the cleanness of my hands
he has rewarded me.
For I have kept the ways of the LORD;
I have not done evil by turning from my God.

PSALM 18:20–21

AS YOU PRAISE GOD TODAY

- Reflect on his promise to reward you when you earnestly seek him.
- Praise God because he is a very great reward.

GOD CANNOT BE CONTAINED

*Will God really dwell on earth? The heavens,
even the highest heaven, cannot contain you.*

1 KINGS 8:27

*Who is able to build a temple for God,
since the heavens, even the highest heavens,
cannot contain him?*

2 CHRONICLES 2:6

As no place can be without God, so no place can
compass and contain him.

STEPHEN CHARNOCK

AS YOU PRAISE GOD TODAY

• Consider how awesome and vast he is that even
the highest heavens cannot contain him. Give
him praise.

• Worship him by saying, "Glory to God in the
highest. I give you glory and honor and praise."

JESUS EXPRESSED EMOTION

As Jesus approached Jerusalem and saw the city,
he wept over it and said, "If you, even you, had
only known on this day what would bring you
peace—but now it is hidden from your eyes."
LUKE 19:41–42

When Jesus saw Mary weeping, and the Jews who
had come along with her also weeping, he was
deeply moved in spirit and troubled. "Where
have you laid Lazarus?" he asked.
"Come and see, Lord," they replied.
Jesus wept.
JOHN 11:33–35

AS YOU PRAISE GOD TODAY

- Praise him for the example Jesus set in showing emotion, yet showing it without sin. Read Hebrews 4:15 and Ephesians 4:26.
- Thank God for making it acceptable to weep. Read Psalm 30:5 and praise him that joy comes in the morning!

JESUS IS A RABBI, TEACHER

*Jesus went throughout Galilee, teaching in their
synagogues, preaching the good news of the
kingdom, and healing every disease
and sickness among the people.*

MATTHEW 4:23

Jesus does it all, and I do nothing, I hold and
know from experience that the kingdom of
heaven is within us. Our Lord needs neither books
nor teachers in order to guide our souls. He, the
teacher of teachers, gives his guidance noiselessly. I
have never heard him speak, and yet I know that he
is within me. At every moment he instructs me and
guides me. And whenever I am in need of it, he
enlightens me afresh.

THERESE OF LISIEUX

AS YOU PRAISE GOD TODAY

- Thank Jesus for all he has taught you through
  his Word and through his Spirit.
- Praise Jesus as the world's greatest teacher who
  taught with authority.
- Thank Jesus for using parables as he taught, so
  you and all people can better relate to and grasp
  his teaching.

JESUS IS THE SON OF GOD

*During the fourth watch of the night Jesus went
out to [his disciples], walking on the lake. . . .
"Lord, if it's you," Peter replied, "tell me to come
to you on the water."
"Come," he said.
Then Peter got down out of the boat, walked
on the water and came toward Jesus. . . .
And when they climbed into the boat,
the wind died down. Then those who were in t
he boat worshiped him, saying, "Truly you are
the Son of God."*
MATTHEW 14:25, 28–29, 32–33

AS YOU PRAISE GOD TODAY

- Reflect on how amazing it is that the God of the
  universe sent his only Son to live among earthly
  people. Praise him for it.

JESUS IS THE SON OF MAN

Jesus said, "When you have lifted up the Son of Man, then you will know that I am the one I claim to be and that I do nothing on my own but speak just what the Father has taught me. The one who sent me is with me; he has not left me alone, for I always do what pleases him."

JOHN 8:28–29

The cross of Christ was triumph for the Son of Man. It was not only a sign that our Lord has triumphed, but that he has triumphed to save the human race. Because of what the Son of Man went through, every human being has been provided with a way of access into the very presence of God.

OSWALD CHAMBERS

AS YOU PRAISE GOD TODAY

- Reflect on this title that Jesus gave himself.
- Praise Jesus for being fully God and also fully human.

KING OF THE JEWS

*After Jesus was born in Bethlehem in Judea,
during the time of King Herod,
Magi from the east came to Jerusalem and asked,
"Where is the one who has been born king
of the Jews? We saw his star in the east
and have come to worship him."*

MATTHEW 2:1–2

*Pilate had a notice prepared and fastened to the
cross. It read: JESUS OF NAZARETH, THE
KING OF THE JEWS. . . . The chief priests of
the Jews protested to Pilate, "Do not write 'The
King of the Jews,' but that this man claimed to be
king of the Jews."
Pilate answered, "What I have written,
I have written."*

JOHN 19:19, 21–22

AS YOU PRAISE GOD TODAY

- Kneel before your King and give him praise.
- Honor him as the King of the Jews.

JESUS IS THE FORGIVER OF SINS

If we confess our sins, [Jesus] is faithful and just and will forgive us our sins and purify us from all unrighteousness.
1 JOHN 1:9

I want you to know that through Jesus the forgiveness of sins is proclaimed to you.
ACTS 13:38

In Christ we have redemption through his blood, the forgiveness of sins, in accordance with the riches of God's grace that he lavished on us with all wisdom and understanding.
EPHESIANS 1:7–8

AS YOU PRAISE GOD TODAY

- Thank Jesus for providing a way to receive forgiveness for your sins.
- Think about how freeing it is to experience forgiveness, and give Jesus praise for making it possible for you.

JESUS IS THE STUMBLING STONE

The LORD Almighty will be a sanctuary;
but for both houses of Israel he will be
a stone that causes men to stumble
and a rock that makes them fall.
And for the people of Jerusalem he will be
a trap and a snare.

ISAIAH 8:14

"See, I lay in Zion a stone that causes
men to stumble
and a rock that makes them fall,
and the one who trusts in him will never
be put to shame."

ROMANS 9:33

AS YOU PRAISE GOD TODAY

- Praise him that you "tripped" over Jesus the Stumbling Stone and received him as your Savior.
- Thank God for revealing to you that righteousness is by faith and not by works.

JESUS IS YOUR FOUNDATION

*No one can lay any foundation other than the
one already laid, which is Jesus Christ.*

1 CORINTHIANS 3:11

Praise to you, our God and Father, for the sure
foundation you have laid for your church. The
cornerstone of hope for your people of old was the
covenant you made with Abraham, that you would
be their God and that they would be your people.
Our cornerstone of hope today is the covenant of
salvation through Jesus Christ. To all who receive
him, to all who believe in his name, he gives them
the right to become the children of God. He is our
foundation, upon this rock you are building your
church. Those of us who trust in him will never be
dismayed.

NIV WORSHIP BIBLE

AS YOU PRAISE GOD TODAY

- Jesus is your foundation, the rock on which your
  life is built. Praise him for being a sure foundation that will never be moved!
- Think of the ways that Christ is the foundation
  of your life and faith.

GOD IS POWERFUL

HA GEVURAH

Christ is not weak in dealing with you, but is powerful among you. For to be sure, he was crucified in weakness, yet he lives by God's power. Likewise, we are weak in him, yet by God's power we will live with him to serve you.

2 CORINTHIANS 13:3–4

Praise God for his acts of power; praise him for his surpassing greatness.

PSALM 150:2

AS YOU PRAISE GOD TODAY

- Think about the verses above and consider the variety of ways God uses his power.
- Magnify him for his great power—power to break strongholds, to heal, to set free, to save, to give life.
- Pray for a revelation of God's power and might. He has all power in heaven and earth.

GOD GIVES YOU JOY

You will go out in joy
and be led forth in peace;
the mountains and hills
will burst into song before you,
and all the trees of the field
will clap their hands.
Isaiah 55:12

Jesus said, "If you obey my commands, you will
remain in my love, just as I have obeyed my
Father's commands and remain in his love. I
have told you this so that my joy may be in you
and that your joy may be complete."
JOHN 15:10–11

AS YOU PRAISE GOD TODAY

- Recall the two or three happiest moments in your life. Joy like that can only come from him. Give God praise for his gift of joy.
- Ask God to drive trouble from your heart and let you bask in the fullness of his joy.

JESUS IS THE SON OF THE MOST HIGH

*The angel said to Mary, "You will be with child
and give birth to a son, and you are to give him
the name Jesus. He will be great and will be
called the Son of the Most High."*

LUKE 1:31–32

*When [the demon-possessed man] saw Jesus from
a distance, he ran and fell on his knees in front of
him. He shouted at the top of his voice, "What do
you want with me, Jesus, Son of the Most High
God? Swear to God that you won't torture me!"
For Jesus had said to him, "Come out of this
man, you evil spirit!"*

MARK 5:6–8

AS YOU PRAISE GOD TODAY

- Thank Jesus for being willing to come down from the Most High to purchase your salvation.
- Give Jesus praise as you think about him being resurrected back to the right hand of the Most High God.
- Even evil spirits cannot stand up to the Son of the Most High. They have to break their hold over those whom Jesus has set free. Give God praise for that wonderful truth!

GOD REJOICES

As a bridegroom rejoices over his bride,
so will your God rejoice over you.
ISAIAH 62:5

The LORD your God is with you,
he is mighty to save.
He will take great delight in you,
he will quiet you with his love,
he will rejoice over you with singing.
ZEPHANIAH 3:17

"I will rejoice in doing [my people] good
and will assuredly plant them in this land
with all my heart and soul."
JEREMIAH 32:41

AS YOU PRAISE GOD TODAY

- Reflect on the verses above and give God praise as you realize how much he rejoices over you.
- Sing a joyful song to God as you realize that he sings over you!

JESUS LOVES CHILDREN

Little children were brought to Jesus for him to place his hands on them and pray for them. But the disciples rebuked those who brought them. Jesus said, "Let the little children come to me, and do not hinder them, for the kingdom of heaven belongs to such as these."

MATTHEW 19:13–14

Jesus said, "Whoever welcomes a little child like this in my name welcomes me. But if anyone causes one of these little ones who believe in me to sin, it would be better for him to have a large millstone hung around his neck and to be drowned in the depths of the sea."

MATTHEW 18:5–6

AS YOU PRAISE GOD TODAY

- Think about how busy Jesus was with all the throngs of people surrounding him, yet he always had time for the children. Praise him for this wonderful attribute.
- In Matthew 18:5-6, Jesus exalts children to his level, and it is obvious he is protective of them. Thank Jesus for demonstrating to us how precious children are.

JESUS IS THE FRIEND OF SINNERS

A man was [in Jericho] by the name of Zacchaeus; he was a chief tax collector and was wealthy. He wanted to see who Jesus was, but being a short man he could not, because of the crowd. So he ran ahead and climbed a sycamore-fig tree to see him, since Jesus was coming that way. When Jesus reached the spot, he looked up and said to him, "Zacchaeus, come down immediately. I must stay at your house today." So he came down at once and welcomed him gladly. All the people saw this and began to mutter, "He has gone to be the guest of a 'sinner.'"
. . . Jesus said to him, "Today salvation has come to this house, because this man, too, is a son of Abraham. For the Son of Man came to seek and to save what was lost."

LUKE 19:5–10

AS YOU PRAISE GOD TODAY

- Rejoice that Jesus was not like the Pharisees, "too good" for sinners. He befriended sinners and led them to repentance and salvation.
- Thank Jesus for loving you when you were a sinner and reaching out to save you.

THE HOLY SPIRIT IS LIKE A FIRE

*John[the Baptist said], "I baptize you with water.
But one more powerful than I will come,
the thongs of whose sandals I am not worthy
to untie. He will baptize you with the
Holy Spirit and with fire."*

LUKE 3:16

To the church, Pentecost brought light, power, joy. There came to each illumination of mind, assurance of heart, intensity of love, fullness of power, exuberance of joy. No one needed to ask if they had received the Holy Ghost. Fire is self-evident. So is power!

SAMUEL CHADWICK

AS YOU PRAISE GOD TODAY

- Thank God for baptizing you not just with water, but with the Holy Spirit.
- Ask him to make your worship more and more spirit-filled.
- Offer up your praise to the Holy Spirit—don't ignore this person of the Trinity.

JESUS IS THE GREAT PHYSICIAN

Christ himself bore our sins in his body on the tree, so that we might die to sins and live for righteousness; by his wounds you have been healed.

1 PETER 2:24

Praise the LORD, O my soul;
all my inmost being, praise his holy name.
Praise the LORD, O my soul,
and forget not all his benefits—
who forgives all your sins
and heals all your diseases.

PSALM 103:1–3

AS YOU PRAISE GOD TODAY

- Praise him that he is the Lord who heals you!
- Thank Jesus for being the Great Physician—for by his wounds you have been healed!

JESUS IS
THE EXPECTED ONE

Rejoice greatly, O Daughter of Zion!
Shout, Daughter of Jerusalem!
See, your king comes to you,
righteous and having salvation,
gentle and riding on a donkey,
on a colt, the foal of a donkey.

ZECHARIAH 9:9

Jesus sent two disciples, saying to them, "Go to the
village ahead of you, and at once you will find a
donkey tied there, with her colt by her. Untie
them and bring them to me. If anyone says
anything to you, tell him that the Lord needs
them, and he will send them right away."

MATTHEW 21:1–3

AS YOU PRAISE GOD TODAY

- Praise him for always fulfilling the things he foretells.
- Rejoice that Jesus is the one who was and is expected.

GOD IS YOUR COMMANDER

Jesus said, "I did not speak of my own accord, but the Father who sent me commanded me what to say and how to say it. I know that his command leads to eternal life. So whatever I say is just what the Father has told me to say."

JOHN 12:49–50

The commands of the LORD are radiant, giving light to the eyes.

PSALM 19:8

This is love for God: to obey his commands.

1 JOHN 5:3

AS YOU PRAISE GOD TODAY

- Thank him for blessing you and causing things to go well for you when you keep his commandments.
- Rejoice! God's commandments are not burdensome, but lead to eternal life.

JESUS IS THE CHOSEN ONE

*While [Peter] was speaking [to Jesus], a cloud
appeared and enveloped them. . . . A voice came
from the cloud, saying, "This is my Son,
whom I have chosen; listen to him."*

LUKE 9:34–35

*"Here is my servant, whom I uphold,
my chosen one in whom I delight;
I will put my Spirit on him
and he will bring justice to the nations,"*

ISAIAH 42:1

AS YOU PRAISE GOD TODAY

- Praise him for choosing Jesus to be your Savior,
  and praise Jesus for accepting the Father's call.
- Read John 15:19 and give praise that just as the
  Father chose Jesus, Jesus has chosen you.

JESUS IS THE DOOR

*Jesus said, "Ask and it will be given to you;
seek and you will find; knock and the door will
be opened to you. For everyone who asks receives;
he who seeks finds; and to him who knocks,
the door will be opened."*

MATTHEW 7:7–8

*Jesus said, "Here I am! I stand at the door
and knock. If anyone hears my voice and
opens the door, I will come in and eat with him,
and he with me."*

REVELATION 3:20

AS YOU PRAISE GOD TODAY

- Praise him for showing you the narrow door and giving you the key: Jesus.
- Thank Jesus for being the door that opens to eternal life.

JESUS IS THE RISEN ONE

*The women [who had come with Jesus from
Galilee] took the spices they had prepared and
went to the tomb. They found the stone rolled
away from the tomb, but when they entered, they
did not find the body of the Lord Jesus. While
they were wondering about this, suddenly two
men in clothes that gleamed like lightning stood
beside them. In their fright the women bowed
down with their faces to the ground, but the men
said to them, "Why do you look for the living
among the dead? He is not here; he has risen!"*

LUKE 24:1–6

*We believe that Jesus died and rose again and so
we believe that God will bring with Jesus those
who have fallen asleep in him.*

1 THESSALONIANS 4:14

AS YOU PRAISE GOD TODAY

- Praise him that he raised Jesus from the dead.
- Rejoice that you will also be raised to eternal life
  if you place your trust in Jesus—the firstborn
  from the dead.

GOD IS THE FATHER
OF ALL LIFE

With you, LORD, is the fountain of life;
in your light we see light.

PSALM 36:9

Praise him, all his angels,
praise him, all his heavenly hosts.
Praise him, sun and moon,
praise him, all you shining stars.
Praise him, you highest heavens
and you waters above the skies.
Let them praise the name of the LORD,
for he commanded and they were created.

PSALM 148:2–5

The God who made the world and everything in
it is the Lord of heaven and earth.

ACTS 17:24

AS YOU PRAISE GOD TODAY

- Rejoice that God is the Father of all life.
- Praise God for the abundant life he has given to all he has created.

JESUS IS THE WORD OF GOD

LOGOS

*In the beginning was the Word, and the Word
was with God, and the Word was God. He was
with God in the beginning.
Though him all things were made; without him
nothing was made that has been made. In him
was life, and that life was the light of men.*

JOHN 1:1–4

*The Word became flesh and made his dwelling
among us. We have seen his glory, the glory
of the One and Only, who came from the Father,
full of grace and truth.*

JOHN 1:14

AS YOU PRAISE GOD TODAY

- Rejoice that Jesus and God's Word are One.
  When you read God's Word, the Bible, it is as
  though Jesus himself were speaking to you.
- Thank God for revealing himself through his
  Word.

JESUS IS THE ONE AND ONLY SON

We have seen his glory, the glory of the One
and Only, who came from the Father,
full of grace and truth.

JOHN 1:14

Jesus said, "God so loved the world that he gave
his one and only Son, that whoever believes in
him shall not perish but have eternal life."

JOHN 3:16

This is how God showed his love among us:
He sent his one and only Son into the world
that we might live through him.

1 JOHN 4:9

AS YOU PRAISE GOD TODAY

- Meditate on the fact that Jesus, your Savior, was the One and Only sacrifice that could be given in your place.
- Praise God for his willingness to give his One and Only Son, the apple of his eye, to gain you as his child.
- Praise Jesus as the One and Only Son who could make the Father known to you.

JESUS IS YOUR BROTHER

Pointing to his disciples, Jesus said, "Here are my mother and my brothers. For whoever does the will of my Father in heaven is my brother and sister and mother."

MATTHEW 12:49–50

Jesus said, "My mother and brothers are those who hear God's word and put it into practice."

LUKE 8:21

Those God foreknew he also predestined to be conformed to the likeness of his Son, that he might be the firstborn among many brothers.

ROMANS 8:29

AS YOU PRAISE GOD TODAY

- Praise him that you have been made a brother to the Lord Jesus Christ.
- Rejoice that you have been made holy, and Jesus is not ashamed to call you a brother.

JESUS GIVES ETERNAL LIFE

*Jesus said, "Whoever drinks the water
I give him will never thirst. Indeed, the water
I give him will become in him a spring
of water welling up to eternal life."*
JOHN 4:14

*Jesus said, "I tell you the truth, whoever hears my
word and believes him who sent me has eternal
life and will not be condemned; he has crossed
over from death to life."*
JOHN 5:24

*Jesus said, "Father, the time has come.
Glorify your Son, that your Son may glorify you.
For you granted him authority over
all people that he might give eternal life to all
those you have given him."*
JOHN 17:1–2

AS YOU PRAISE GOD TODAY

- Praise Jesus for giving you eternal life rather than eternal condemnation.
- Rejoice that you will live forever with Jesus!
- Thank Jesus for the spring of water that wells up within you to eternal life.

JESUS IS THE PROPHET

*The LORD said, "I will raise up for [my people]
a prophet like [Moses] from among their brothers;
I will put my words in his mouth, and he will
tell them everything I command him."*

DEUTERONOMY 18:18

*Jesus went up and touched the coffin, and those
carrying it stood still. He said, "Young man, I say
to you, get up!" The dead man sat up and began
to talk, and Jesus gave him back to his mother.
They were all filled with awe and praised God.
"A great prophet has appeared among us,"
they said. "God has come to help his people."*

LUKE 7:14–16

*After the people saw the miraculous sign that
Jesus did, they began to say, "Surely this is the
Prophet who is to come into the world."*

JOHN 6:14

AS YOU PRAISE GOD TODAY

• Praise God for sending Jesus, the Prophet, just
as he said he would.

JESUS IS THE LAMB OF GOD

*You know that it was not with perishable things
such as silver or gold that you were redeemed
from the empty way of life handed down to you
from your forefathers, but with the precious blood
of Christ, a lamb without blemish or defect.*

1 PETER 1:18–19

*John saw Jesus coming toward him and said,
"Look, the Lamb of God, who takes away
the sin of the world!"*

JOHN 1:29

*In a loud voice [many angels] sang:
"Worthy is the Lamb, who was slain,
to receive power and wealth
and wisdom and strength
and honor and glory and praise!"*

REVELATION 5:12

AS YOU PRAISE GOD TODAY

- Praise Jesus for being the perfect Lamb, without
  blemish or defect, who was slain to take away
  your sin.
- Worship the Lamb of God, singing the song the
  angels sang in Revelation 5:12.

JESUS WAS KNOWN AS THE SON OF JOSEPH

*When Joseph woke up, he did what the angel
of the Lord had commanded him
and took Mary home as his wife. But he had
no union with her until she gave birth to a son.
And he gave him the name Jesus.*

MATTHEW 1:24–25

*Now Jesus himself was about thirty years old
when he began his ministry. He was the son,
so it was thought, of Joseph.*

LUKE 3:23

AS YOU PRAISE GOD TODAY

- Praise Jesus for his humanity. Because of it, he can relate to you.
- Praise Jesus for his divinity. Because of it, he opened the way for your personal relationship with God.

JESUS OF NAZARETH

*Men of Israel, listen to this: Jesus of Nazareth
was a man accredited by God to you by miracles,
wonders and signs, which God did among
you through him, as you yourselves know.*

ACTS 2:22

*You know what has happened throughout
Judea, beginning in Galilee after the baptism
that John preached— how God anointed Jesus
of Nazareth with the Holy Spirit and power,
and how he went around doing good and healing
all who were under the power of the devil,
because God was with him.*

ACTS 10:37–38

AS YOU PRAISE GOD TODAY

- Rejoice that Jesus of Nazareth is a miracle worker.
- Praise God for anointing Jesus of Nazareth with
  the Holy Spirit and power so Jesus could do
  good and heal all who were oppressed.

THE HOLY SPIRIT IS LIKE THE WIND

Jesus said, "The wind blows wherever it pleases. You hear its sound, but you cannot tell where it comes from or where it is going. So it is with everyone born of the Spirit."

JOHN 3:8

Without the power of the Holy Spirit all human efforts, methods, and plans are as futile as attempting to propel a boat by puffing at the sails with our own breath.

AS YOU PRAISE GOD TODAY

- Remember when you feel the wind blow that God's Spirit is all around you.
- Praise him for sending the Holy Spirit to fill your sail like a wind, propelling you toward the destination he intends for you.

GOD IS CONCERNED
ABOUT DETAIL

*Jesus said, "Are not five sparrows sold for two
pennies? Yet not one of them is forgotten by God.
Indeed, the very hairs of your head are all
numbered. Don't be afraid; you are worth
more than many sparrows."*

LUKE 12:6–7

*Lift your eyes and look to the heavens:
Who created all these?
He who brings out the starry host one by one,
and calls them each by name.
Because of his great power and mighty strength,
not one of them is missing.*

ISAIAH 40:26

AS YOU PRAISE GOD TODAY

• Praise him that he knows you so intimately,
down to the number of hairs on your head.

• Thank God for loving you so much that he has
a list of all the tears you have shed.

THE LORD IS GENTLE

*Jesus said, "Take my yoke upon you and learn
from me, for I am gentle and humble in heart,
and you will find rest for your souls."*

MATTHEW 11:29

*The LORD tends his flock like a shepherd:
He gathers the lambs in his arms
and carries them close to his heart;
he gently leads those that have young.*

ISAIAH 40:11

AS YOU PRAISE GOD TODAY

- Praise Jesus for being gentle and not harsh with you.
- Thank him for the times he has dealt gently with you.

JESUS IS THE SAVIOR OF THE WORLD

"God did not send his Son into the world to condemn the world, but to save the world through him."

JOHN 3:17

Jesus said, "I did not come to judge the world, but to save it."

JOHN 12:47

Let us fix our eyes on the blood of Christ and understand how precious it is to his Father, because, being poured out forever for our salvation, it won for the whole world the grace of repentance.

CLEMENT OF ROME

AS YOU PRAISE GOD TODAY

- Consider what "the whole world" means, and thank Jesus for coming as the Savior for the entire human race—that means all people, from all over the world, throughout time.
- Thank Jesus for being your Savior.

JESUS IS THE BREAD OF HEAVEN

Jesus said, "I tell you the truth, it is not Moses who has given you the bread from heaven, but it is my Father who gives you the true bread from heaven. The bread of God is he who comes down from heaven and gives life to the world."

JOHN 6:32–33

During the Israelites' term of wandering in the wilderness, every day for forty years God sent manna, a white miracle bread that "tasted like wafers made with honey" to satisfy the people's physical hunger and nutritional needs.

In this New Testament verse, Jesus offers himself as the "bread of life," available to permanently satisfy our spiritual hunger. Each day, by engaging in prayer and the reading of God's Word, we can be confident of receiving spiritual sustenance from our Life Giver.

LIFE PROMISES BIBLE

AS YOU PRAISE GOD TODAY

- Praise Jesus for being the Bread of Heaven. Once you partake of him, you are satisfied forever.
- Praise God for always looking out for your needs. The Israelites needed physical food in the desert, and he gave it to them. You need spiritual food, and he gives it to you.

GOD IS A WARRIOR

The LORD is a warrior;
the LORD is his name.
Pharaoh's chariots and his army
he has hurled into the sea.
EXODUS 15:3–4

The LORD will march out like a mighty man,
like a warrior he will stir up his zeal;
with a shout he will raise the battle cry
and will triumph over his enemies.
ISAIAH 42:13

The LORD is with me like a mighty warrior;
so my persecutors will stumble and not prevail.
JEREMIAH 20:11

AS YOU PRAISE GOD TODAY

- Praise God because he always triumphs over his enemies.
- Praise God for being a mighty warrior who fights on your behalf.

GOD IS YOUR AVENGER

*Do not take revenge, my friends, but leave room
for God's wrath, for it is written: "It is mine
to avenge; I will repay," says the Lord.*

ROMANS 12:19

*"When I sharpen my flashing sword
and my hand grasps it in judgment,
I will take vengeance on my adversaries
and repay those who hate me," says the LORD.*

DEUTERONOMY 32:41

*The LORD lives! Praise be to my Rock!
Exalted be God my Savior!
He is the God who avenges me.*

PSALM 18:46–47

AS YOU PRAISE GOD TODAY

• Praise him that you need not avenge yourself.
God has promised to do that for you!

JESUS IS LIVING WATER

Jesus said, "Whoever drinks the water I give him
will never thirst. Indeed, the water I give him
will become in him a spring of water
welling up to eternal life."
JOHN 4:14

The Israelites understood the difference between "living water" and "dead water," being familiar with the Dead Sea that stretches some fifty miles. Its waters settle at the earth's lowest point and contain a high concentration of salt and minerals that prevents the existence of organic life. Ezekiel prophesied (Ezekiel 47:9) that this sea would come to life as the river of God flows into it. Once again God promises to bring life from death.

As we allow God's river to flow though us, he regenerates the dead places within us. God's words foster life and blessing.

LIFE PROMISES BIBLE

AS YOU PRAISE GOD TODAY

- Thank him for giving you living, spiritual water so pure and so powerful that you will never be thirsty again.

JESUS IS THE LIGHT OF THE WORLD

When Jesus spoke again to the people, he said, "I am the light of the world. Whoever follows me will never walk in darkness, but will have the light of life."
JOHN 8:12

I am a believer in Jesus and his promises: . . . his word a lamp unto my feet guiding my every step; his eyes seeing for me when I am too blind to see; his fire setting my heart ablaze so that I can see my sin and allow his love to consume it. The sweet glow of his presence shines into my darkness. And as I have received, I can give.

KATHY TROCCOLI

AS YOU PRAISE GOD TODAY

- Thank him for the light that shines in darkness —his Word and his presence.
- Praise God that with Jesus you need never walk in darkness. Personalize John 8:12, stating that Jesus is the light of your world.

JESUS IS THE TRUTH

*Jesus said, "I am the way and the truth and the life.
No one comes to the Father except through me."*
JOHN 14:6

*The Word became flesh and made his dwelling
among us. We have seen his glory, the glory of
the One and Only, who came from the Father,
full of grace and truth.*
JOHN 1:14

*Jesus said, "You are right in saying I am a king.
In fact, for this reason I was born, and for this
I came into the world, to testify to the truth.
Everyone on the side of truth listens to me."*
JOHN 18:37

AS YOU PRAISE GOD TODAY

- Praise him as you consider that not only does
  God testify to the truth, he is full of truth and
  actually is truth.
- Praise God for always speaking the truth. Jesus
  said "I tell you the truth" seventy-eight times in
  the four Gospels.

GOD IS TRUSTWORTHY

God is truthful.
JOHN 3:33

O Sovereign LORD, you are God!
Your words are trustworthy.
2 SAMUEL 7:28

The word of the LORD is right and true;
he is faithful in all he does.
PSALM 33:4

AS YOU PRAISE GOD TODAY

- Praise him for being utterly trustworthy. People may let you down, but God never will.
- Think about the fact that it is impossible for God to lie. Praise him for the security you feel as you ponder this truth.

JESUS TEACHES US HOW TO PRAY

"This, then, is how you should pray:
'Our Father in heaven,
hallowed be your name,
your kingdom come,
your will be done
on earth as it is in heaven.
Give us today our daily bread.
Forgive us our debts,
as we also have forgiven our debtors.
And lead us not into temptation,
but deliver us from the evil one.'"

MATTHEW 6:9–13

AS YOU PRAISE GOD TODAY

- Praise Jesus for teaching you how to pray. You can read about this above and in John 17 where one of his actual prayers is recorded.
- Thank God for revealing to you some of the intimate communication he and Jesus shared.
- Praise Jesus for interceding for you.

GOD DESIRES
YOUR PRAISE

*Jesus said, "A time is coming and has now
come when the true worshipers will worship
the Father in spirit and truth, for they are
the kind of worshipers the Father seeks."*
JOHN 4:23

*"I desire mercy, not sacrifice,
and acknowledgment of God rather than
burnt offerings."*
HOSEA 6:6

*"He who sacrifices thank offerings honors me,
and he prepares the way
so that I may show him the salvation of God."*
PSALM 50:23

AS YOU PRAISE GOD TODAY

- Praise God as you acknowledge him in all things.
- Honor God by sacrificing a thank offering
  to him.
- Praise him as the One and only God you serve,
  having no other gods before him.

GOD IS GOOD

The LORD is good and his love endures forever;
his faithfulness continues through all generations.

PSALM 100:5

The LORD is good to all;
he has compassion on all he has made.
All you have made will praise you, O LORD;
your saints will extol you.

PSALM 145:9–10

The LORD is good to those whose hope is in him,
to the one who seeks him.

LAMENTATIONS 3:25

AS YOU PRAISE GOD TODAY

- Think of the many ways God has been good to you, and give him praise for them.
- You need never be afraid of God for he is good all the time. Rejoice!

JESUS IS THE RESURRECTION AND THE LIFE

Jesus said, "I am the resurrection and the life. He who believes in me will live, even though he dies."
JOHN 11:25

We know that the one who raised the Lord Jesus from the dead will also raise us with Jesus and present us with you in his presence.
2 CORINTHIANS 4:14

God's most profound word to us is this: LIFE. It is his desire that no one should perish but that all his children should live. He calls us from dying to living.

WALTER WANGERIN, JR.

AS YOU PRAISE GOD TODAY

- Praise him that just as Jesus' body was brought forth from the grave, your body also will be resurrected.
- Because of God, you are not just marking time in a meaningless existence. If you have Jesus, you have life.
- Praise him that you can never really die.
- Ask God to help you to live for him, rather than for yourself.

JESUS IS THE WAY

Thomas said to Jesus,
"Lord, we don't know where you are going,
so how can we know the way?"
Jesus answered, "I am the way and the truth
and the life. No one comes to the Father
except through me."

JOHN 14:5–6

The way to Jesus is not by Cambridge and Oxford, Glasgow, Edinburgh, London, Princeton, Harvard, Yale, Socrates, Plato, Shakespeare or the poets. It is over an old-fashioned hill called Calvary.

GIPSY SMITH

AS YOU PRAISE GOD TODAY

- Praise Jesus for being the way to the Father and for revealing it to you.
- Bring him praise by explaining to others that Jesus is the way to eternal life.

GOD IS YOUR COUNSELOR

I am always with you;
you hold me by my right hand, O Lord.
You guide me with your counsel,
and afterward you will take me into glory.

Psalm 73:23–24

"I will ask the Father, and he will give you
another Counselor to be with you forever—the
Spirit of truth. The world cannot accept him,
because it neither sees him nor knows him."

John 14:16–17

The people who related to God best—Abraham, Moses, David, Isaiah, Jeremiah —treated him with startling familiarity. They talked to God as if he were sitting in a chair beside them, as one might talk to a counselor, a boss, a parent, or a lover. They treated him like a person.

Philip Yancey

AS YOU PRAISE GOD TODAY

- Praise God for the ways you have sensed his counsel in your life.
- Give him glory for being wonderful in counsel and magnificent in wisdom.

JESUS IS THE HOLY ONE

*Simon Peter said to Jesus, "We believe and know
that you are the Holy One of God."*
JOHN 6:69

*My heart is glad and my tongue rejoices;
my body also will rest secure,
because you will not abandon me
to the grave, nor will you let your
Holy One see decay.*
PSALM 16:9–10

AS YOU PRAISE GOD TODAY

- Rejoice that the Holy One who was promised was Jesus, the Son of God.
- Praise God for not allowing his Holy One to remain in the grave, but raised him up in triumph.
- Thank him that you have an anointing from the Holy One because you have accepted Jesus.

KING OF KINGS AND LORD OF LORDS

God, the blessed and only Ruler, the King of kings and Lord of lords, who alone is immortal and who lives in unapproachable light, whom no one has seen or can see. To him be honor and might forever. Amen.

1 TIMOTHY 6:15–16

The LORD your God is God of gods and Lord of lords, the great God, mighty and awesome.

DEUTERONOMY 10:17

AS YOU PRAISE GOD TODAY

- Think about all the kings of the earth being subject to Jesus, the King of all kings. Give him a shout of praise!
- Give thanks to the Lord of lords: His love endures forever (Psalms 136:3).

JESUS IS THE VINE

Jesus said, "I am the vine; you are the branches. If a man remains in me and I in him, he will bear much fruit; apart from me you can do nothing."
JOHN 15:5

Without the vine the branch can do nothing. To the vine it owes its right of place in the vineyard, its life, and its fruitfulness. And so the Lord says, "Apart from me you can do nothing." The believer can each day be pleasing to God only in that which he does through the power of Christ dwelling in him. The daily inflowing of the life-sap of the Holy Spirit is his only power to bring forth the fruit. He lives fully in him and is for each moment dependent on him alone.

ANDREW MURRAY

AS YOU PRAISE GOD TODAY

- Praise the True Vine for sending you the Holy Spirit, who causes you to grow little by little each day.
- Praise Jesus as the Vine who works through you, one of his branches.

GOD IS THE GARDENER

The man who plants and the man who waters
have one purpose, and each will be rewarded
according to his own labor. For we are God's fel-
low workers; you are God's field, God's building.

1 CORINTHIANS 3:8–9

Jesus used many analogies from nature in teaching parables. Think of how a gardener tends the plants in his care. He diligently tills and prepares the soil, gently inserts various plants into to ground, and then faithfully fertilizes and waters the treasures he is cultivating. . . .

On a broader scale, the Gardener also cultivates the kingdom of God. He patiently tends his crop until the time of harvest has come. Rejoice as you see the fullness of time approaching. Harvest day is coming!

AS YOU PRAISE GOD TODAY

- Praise him for working in your life like a gardener works in his garden, tilling the ground, pulling weeds, fertilizing, watering, and harvesting.
- Rejoice as you see the time of harvest approaching.

SPIRIT OF TRUTH

*Jesus said, "I will ask the Father, and he will
give you another Counselor to be with you
forever—the Spirit of truth. The world cannot
accept him, because it neither sees him
nor knows him. But you know him,
for he lives with you and will be in you."*

JOHN 14:16–17

*Come, Holy Ghost, for moved by thee
The prophet wrote and spoke;
Unlock the Truth, thyself the key,
Unseal the sacred book.*

JOHN CALVIN

AS YOU PRAISE GOD TODAY

- Praise him that no matter what persuasive arguments or earnest claims someone might make, the Spirit of Truth is inside your heart, helping you to discern the truth.

- Praise God that he is Truth. In a desert of lies, the Truth is like a glistening stream. In this world, how precious it is to take a cooling drink of Truth.

JESUS IS THE SANCTIFIER

*You were washed, you were sanctified, you were
justified in the name of the Lord Jesus Christ
and by the Spirit of our God.*

1 CORINTHIANS 6:11

*Jesus prayed, "Sanctify [my disciples] by the truth;
your word is truth. . . . For them I sanctify myself,
that they too may be truly sanctified."*

JOHN 17:17, 19

*May God himself, the God of peace, sanctify you
through and through. May your whole spirit,
soul and body be kept blameless at the coming
of our Lord Jesus Christ.*

1 THESSALONIANS 5:23

AS YOU PRAISE GOD TODAY

- Praise him that he sanctifies you through and
  through—spirit, soul, and body.
- Rejoice that you are sanctified by the Spirit
  of God.

JESUS IS COURAGEOUS

Jesus said, "Father, if you are willing, take this cup from me; yet not my will, but yours be done."
LUKE 22:42

*I offered my back to those who beat me,
my cheeks to those who pulled out my beard;
I did not hide my face
from mocking and spitting.
Because the Sovereign LORD helps me,
I will not be disgraced.
Therefore have I set my face like flint,
and I know I will not be put to shame.*
ISAIAH 50:6–7

Let us fix our eyes on Jesus, the author and perfecter of our faith, who for the joy set before him endured the cross, scorning its shame, and sat down at the right hand of the throne of God.
HEBREWS 12:2

AS YOU PRAISE GOD TODAY

- Praise Jesus for performing the ultimate act of courage by bearing your sin on the cross.
- Worship and honor Jesus for choosing the Father's will over his own.

GOD IS THE GIVER
OF LIFE

*The LORD God formed the man
from the dust of the ground and breathed
into his nostrils the breath of life,
and the man became a living being.*

GENESIS 2:7

*In God's hand is the life of every creature
and the breath of all mankind.*

JOB 12:10

*The Spirit of God has made me;
the breath of the Almighty gives me life.*

JOB 33:4

AS YOU PRAISE GOD TODAY

- Praise him that although your earthly breath
  will someday cease, you've already received the
  breath of heaven, the true breath that will
  never fail.
- Praise God for creating and giving life to you
  and all living beings.

GOD SITS ON HIS THRONE

I was in the Spirit, and there before me was a throne in heaven with someone sitting on it. And the one who sat there had the appearance of jasper and carnelian. A rainbow, resembling an emerald, encircled the throne.

REVELATION 4:2–3

Whenever the living creatures give glory, honor and thanks to him who sits on the throne and who lives for ever and ever, the twenty-four elders fall down before him who sits on the throne, and worship him who lives for ever and ever. They lay their crowns before the throne and say: "You are worthy, our Lord and God, to receive glory and honor and power, for you created all things, and by your will they were created and have their being."

REVELATION 4:9–11

AS YOU PRAISE GOD TODAY

- Praise God for giving you a glimpse of his glory through the verses above.
- Thank him that although he rules with such majesty, God invites you to boldly approach his throne at any time.

THE HOLY SPIRIT
IS A SEAL

*You also were included in Christ when you heard
the word of truth, the gospel of your salvation.
Having believed, you were marked in him with
a seal, the promised Holy Spirit,
who is a deposit guaranteeing our inheritance
until the redemption of those who are God's
possession—to the praise of his glory.*
EPHESIANS 1:13–14

*God set his seal of ownership on us,
and put his Spirit in our hearts as a deposit,
guaranteeing what is to come.*
2 CORINTHIANS 1:22

AS YOU PRAISE GOD TODAY

- Rejoice that whatever joy you've already received from the Lord is just a fraction of the joys to come.
- Rejoice that you have been marked with the seal of the Holy Spirit and the enemy has no claim to you now.
- Praise God that he puts his seal on all who belong to him, guaranteeing his children entrance into heaven.

GOD TENDS AND CARES FOR HIS CREATION

God makes grass grow for the cattle,
and plants for man to cultivate—
bringing forth food from the earth: . . .
The trees of the LORD are well watered,
the cedars of Lebanon that he planted.
PSALM 104:14, 16

Jesus said, "Why do you worry about clothes? See
how the lilies of the field grow. They do not labor
or spin. Yet I tell you that not even Solomon in
all his splendor was dressed like one of these.
If that is how God clothes the grass of the field,
which is here today and tomorrow is thrown into
the fire, will he not much more clothe you,
O you of little faith?"
MATTHEW 6:28–30

AS YOU PRAISE GOD TODAY

- Give him praise for cultivating the vegetation of the earth for all of his creatures—including you.
- Thank God for sending the rain so that the grass and other plants will grow.

JESUS SENDS YOU

*Jesus said, "Peace be with you! As the Father
has sent me, I am sending you."*
JOHN 20:21

*Jesus said, "Go and make disciples of all nations,
baptizing them in the name of the Father
and of the Son and of the Holy Spirit,
and teaching them to obey everything I have
commanded you. And surely I am with
you always, to the very end of the age."*
MATTHEW 28:19–20

*Jesus said to[his disciples], "Go into all the world
and preach the good news to all creation.
Whoever believes and is baptized will be saved."*
MARK 16:15–16

AS YOU PRAISE GOD TODAY

- Give Jesus praise for trusting you enough to send you to do his work on earth.
- Thank Jesus for the privilege of serving him.
- Praise Jesus for not sending you out alone to do his work—he is with you always.

JESUS OBEYED THE FATHER

*Jesus said, "I did not speak of my own accord,
but the Father who sent me commanded me
what to say and how to say it."*
JOHN 12:49

*Jesus said, "If you obey my commands, you will
remain in my love, just as I have obeyed my
Father's commands and remain in his love."*
JOHN 15:10

*Being found in appearance as a man,
Jesus humbled himself
and became obedient to death—
even death on a cross!
Therefore God exalted him to the highest place
and gave him the name that is above every name.*
PHILIPPIANS 2:8–9

AS YOU PRAISE GOD TODAY

- Praise Jesus for the wonderful example he set for
  us when he chose to obey his Father.
- Rejoice that as you obey Jesus the way he obeyed
  the Father, you will feel anchored by his love.

THE GOD OF
OUR FATHERS

*We cried out to the LORD, the God of our fathers,
and the LORD heard our voice and saw our
misery, toil and oppression. So the LORD brought
us out of Egypt with a mighty hand and an
outstretched arm, with great terror and with
miraculous signs and wonders.*

DEUTERONOMY 26:7–8

Throughout the generations, the Jews looked forward to the coming Messiah, the One to ultimately fulfill the covenant made by the God of their fathers. Imagine the impact Peter, Ananais, and the other believers had on their fellow Jews when they declared that the God of their fathers had raised Jesus from the dead and had glorified him. Think of how Saul must have felt that the God of his fathers had chosen *him* to see the Righteous One and hear words from his mouth! There was great cause for rejoicing!

AS YOU PRAISE GOD TODAY

- Praise him for fulfilling the covenant he made with Abraham, Isaac, and Jacob when he sent Jesus into the world.

SPIRIT OF WISDOM

A shoot will come up from the stump of Jesse;
from his roots a Branch will bear fruit.
The Spirit of the LORD will rest on him—
the Spirit of wisdom and of understanding,
the Spirit of counsel and of power,
the Spirit of knowledge and of the fear
of the LORD—
and he will delight in the fear of the LORD.
ISAIAH 11:1–3

I keep asking that the God of our Lord Jesus
Christ, the glorious Father, may give you
the Spirit of wisdom and revelation,
so that you may know him better.
EPHESIANS 1:17

AS YOU PRAISE GOD TODAY

- Praise him for the Spirit of Wisdom that rests on Jesus.
- Thank God for answering Paul's prayer and giving you the Spirit of Wisdom.

JESUS IS THE JUDGE OF THE LIVING AND THE DEAD

Christ commanded us to preach to the people and to testify that he is the one whom God appointed as judge of the living and the dead.

ACTS 10:42

In the presence of God and of Christ Jesus, who will judge the living and the dead, and in view of his appearing and his kingdom, I give you this charge: Preach the Word; be prepared in season and out of season; correct, rebuke and encourage —with great patience and careful instruction.

2 TIMOTHY 4:1–2

It is the Lord who judges me. Therefore judge nothing before the appointed time; wait till the Lord comes. He will bring to light what is hidden in darkness and will expose the motives of men's hearts. At that time each will receive his praise from God.

1 CORINTHIANS 4:4–5

AS YOU PRAISE GOD TODAY

- Read 1 John 1:7–9 and praise God for giving you the opportunity to confess your sin and be cleansed.

THE SPIRIT OF JESUS

*I know that through your prayers and the help
given by the Spirit of Jesus Christ, what has happened to me will turn out for my deliverance. I
eagerly expect and hope that I will in no way be
ashamed, but will have sufficient courage so that
now as always Christ will be exalted in my body,
whether by life or by death. For to me, to live is
Christ and to die is gain.*

PHILIPPIANS 1:19–21

*This is the one who came by water and blood—
Jesus Christ. He did not come by water only, but
by water and blood. And it is the Spirit who
testifies, because the Spirit is the truth.*

1 JOHN 5:6

AS YOU PRAISE GOD TODAY

- Thank God for the Spirit of Jesus who helps you
  as he helped the Apostle Paul.
- Praise God for giving you the Spirit of Jesus to
  intervene when you are about to do something
  that would not be pleasing to him.

THE "UNKNOWN" GOD

Since the creation of the world God's invisible
qualities—his eternal power and divine
nature—have been clearly seen,
being understood from what has been made,
so that men are without excuse.

ROMANS 1:20

For as I [Paul] walked around and looked
carefully at [the Athenians'] objects of worship,
I even found an altar with this inscription:
TO AN UNKNOWN GOD. *Now what you*
worship as something unknown I am going
to proclaim to you.

ACTS 17:23

AS YOU PRAISE GOD TODAY

- Praise God for planting reminders of himself everywhere so that no one can ignore his existence.
- Rejoice that he is not an unknown to you— through Jesus, he has made himself known.

GOD IS THE DIVINE BEING

*God's divine power has given us everything we need
for life and godliness through our knowledge of him
who called us by his own glory and goodness.
Through these he has given us his very great and
precious promises, so that through them you may
participate in the divine nature and escape the corruption in the world caused by evil desires.*

2 PETER 1:3–4

In our society, people have made gods out of fame,
wealth, beauty, or addictions.

Imagine bowing down to a golden statue or
some other image representing a god; think of the
futility of praying to such a man-made object, which
is incapable of responding in any way. Compare that
to the awesome privilege of experiencing two-way
communication with God Almighty, the Divine
Being who created you and everything in the
universe. That is something to rejoice about!

AS YOU PRAISE GOD TODAY

- Praise God that he is not an image made by
  man, but is the Divine Being who has neither
  beginning nor end.
- Praise him for making his divine power available
  to you.

THE SPIRIT OF HOLINESS

Ascribe to the LORD the glory due his name;
worship the LORD in the splendor of his holiness.
PSALMS 29:2

God's holiness is the foundation on which the whole universe rests. If he ever did anything that was selfish or unjust, everything would begin to fall apart. But God, with all his power and other unlimited abilities, has never done anything wrong, and he never will do anything wrong. We will always be able to trust him, and he will always inspire us to pray and work to be holy—because he is holy.

CHRISTIAN GROWTH STUDY BIBLE

AS YOU PRAISE GOD TODAY

• Praise God for his holiness, which holds the universe together.

JESUS IS YOUR COMFORTER

*Praise be to the God and Father of our Lord Jesus
Christ, the Father of compassion and the God of
all comfort, who comforts us in all our troubles,
so that we can comfort those in any trouble with
the comfort we ourselves have received from God.*

2 CORINTHIANS 1:3–4

*The Spirit of the Sovereign LORD is on me,
because the Lord has anointed me . . .
to comfort all who mourn,
and provide for those who grieve in Zion—
to bestow on them a crown of beauty
instead of ashes,
the oil of gladness
instead of mourning,
and a garment of praise
instead of a spirit of despair.*

ISAIAH 61:1–3

AS YOU PRAISE GOD TODAY

- Praise Jesus for comforting you so you can comfort others.
- Thank Jesus for comforting you when you mourn, and for giving you the oil of gladness and a garment of praise.

THE HOLY SPIRIT IS YOUR COUNSELOR

Jesus said, "I will ask the Father, and he will give you another Counselor to be with you forever."
JOHN 14:16

Jesus said, "The Counselor, the Holy Spirit, whom the Father will send in my name, will teach you all things and will remind you of everything I have said to you."
JOHN 14:26

The word "Counselor" in the verses above comes from the Greek word *paraklētŏs*. According to *Strong's Exhaustive Concordance*, this word could be translated as "An *intercessor, consoler:*—advocate, comforter." In short, whenever you need someone to come alongside to help you, the Holy Spirit has been sent to fill that role.

AS YOU PRAISE GOD TODAY

• Thank Jesus for sending the Counselor to you.
• Rejoice that the Holy Spirit is available to you at all times to help you with your every need.

JESUS IS A RULER

"This is what the prophet has written:
"'But you, Bethlehem, in the land of Judah,
are by no means least among the rulers of Judah;
for out of you will come a ruler
who will be the shepherd of my people Israel.'"
MATTHEW 2:5–6

Grace and peace to you from him who is, and
who was, and who is to come, and from the seven
spirits before his throne, and from Jesus Christ,
who is the faithful witness, the firstborn from the
dead, and the ruler of the kings of the earth.
REVELATION 1:4–5

AS YOU PRAISE GOD TODAY

- Revere and honor Jesus as the ruler of creation and the ruler of the kings of the earth.
- Give him glory and praise because all things were created by him and for him, including the rulers of the earth.

THE HOLY SPIRIT LEADS

*Those who are led by the Spirit of God
are sons of God.*
ROMANS 8:14

*Jesus said, "When he, the Spirit of truth, comes,
he will guide you into all truth. He will not
speak on his own; he will speak only what he
hears, and he will tell you what is yet to come."*
JOHN 16:13

The mind controlled by the Spirit is life and peace.
ROMANS 8:6

No generation can claim to have plumbed to the depths the unfathomable riches of Christ. The Holy Spirit has promised to lead us step by step into the fullness of truth.

LEON JOSEPH SUENENS

AS YOU PRAISE GOD TODAY

- Thank him that you don't have to walk through life alone for God's Spirit leads you in the way you should go.
- Thank the Holy Spirit for guiding and leading you into all truth.

THE SPIRIT OF CHRIST

If Christ is in you, your body is dead because of
sin, yet your sprit is alive because of righteousness.
And if the Spirit of him who raised Jesus from the
dead is living in you, he who raised Christ from
the dead will also give life to your mortal bodies
through his Spirit, who lives in you.

ROMANS 8:10–11

Lord Jesus, Christ, be present now,
Our hearts in true devotion bow,
Thy Spirit send with grace divine,
And let Thy truth within us shine.

WILHELM II, DUKE OF SACHSEN-WEIMAR

AS YOU PRAISE GOD TODAY

- Thank Jesus for sending his Spirit to live within
  you.

DADDY

ABBA

[Jesus] fell to the ground and prayed that if possible the hour[of his crucifixtion] might pass from him. "Abba, Father," he said, "everything is possible for you. Take this cup from me. Yet not what I will, but what you will."

MARK 14:35–36

You did not receive a spirit that makes you a slave again to fear, but you received the Spirit of sonship. And by him we cry, "Abba, Father."

ROMANS 8:15

Because you are sons, God sent the Spirit of his Son into our hearts, the Spirit who calls out, "Abba, Father." So you are no longer a slave, but a son.

GALATIANS 4:6–7

AS YOU PRAISE GOD TODAY

- Think of all the ways God has been a tender daddy to you. Thank him and praise him that he has allowed you to call him Abba.
- Praise God that just like Jesus referred to him as Daddy, you can, too.

JESUS IS THE MORNING STAR

*"I, Jesus, have sent my angel to give you
this testimony for the churches. I am the
Root and the Offspring of David,
and the bright Morning Star."*

REVELATION 22:16

*The Lord said, "This is my Son, whom I love;
with him I am well pleased." We ourselves heard
this voice that came from heaven when we were
with him on the sacred mountain.
We have the word of the prophets made more certain, and you will do well to pay attention to it,
as to a light shining in a dark place, until the day
dawns and the morning star rises in your hearts.*

2 PETER 1:17–19

Christ is the Morning Star who, when the night
of this world is past, brings to his saints the
promise of the light of life and opens everlasting day.

VENERABLE BEDE

AS YOU PRAISE GOD TODAY

• Praise Jesus that he is the bright Morning Star
who reigns in your life no matter how dark your
situation.

GOD IS THE SOURCE OF WISDOM

Oh, the depth of the riches of the wisdom
and knowledge of God!
How unsearchable his judgments,
and his paths beyond tracing out!

ROMANS 11:33

If any of you lacks wisdom, he should ask God,
who gives generously to all without finding fault,
and it will be given to him.

JAMES 1:5

The life built on the wisdom of God endures forever ... Wisdom is for the asking.

CHARLES STANLEY

AS YOU PRAISE GOD TODAY

• Thank God that his wisdom is available to you; all you have to do is ask.

THE NAME OF THE LORD IS GREAT

The name of the LORD is a strong tower;
the righteous run to it and are safe.
PROVERBS 18:10

"My name will be great among the nations, from
the rising to the setting of the sun. In every place
incense and pure offerings will be brought to my
name, because my name will be great among the
nations," says the LORD Almighty.
MALACHI 1:11

For the sake of his great name the LORD will not
reject his people, because the LORD was pleased
to make you his own.
1 SAMUEL 12:22

AS YOU PRAISE GOD TODAY

- Bless his great name.
- Praise God because he is a strong tower to you;
  you can run to him and be safe.

THE HOLY SPIRIT GIVES GIFTS

Now to each one the manifestation of the Spirit is given for the common good. To one there is given through the Spirit the message of wisdom, to another the message of knowledge by means of the same Spirit, to another faith by the same Spirit, to another gifts of healing by that one Spirit, to another miraculous powers, to another prophecy, to another distinguishing between spirits, to another speaking in different kinds of tongues, and to still another the interpretation of tongues. All these are the work of one and the same Spirit, and he gives them to each one, just as he determines.

1 CORINTHIANS 12:7–11

Religious work can be done by natural men without the gifts of the Spirit, and it can be done well and skillfully. But work designed for eternity can only be done by the eternal Spirit.

A. W. TOZER

AS YOU PRAISE GOD TODAY

- Rejoice in the many gifts that God has given you in the Holy Spirit.
- Thank him for each of those gifts listed in 1 Corinthians 12.

GOD CONTROLS THE WEATHER

The LORD does whatever pleases him,
in the heavens and on the earth,
in the seas and all their depths.
He makes clouds rise from the ends of the earth;
he sends lightning with the rain
and brings out the wind from his storehouses.

PSALM 135:6–7

God covers the sky with clouds;
he supplies the earth with rain. . . .
He spreads the snow like wool
and scatters the frost like ashes. . . .
He sends his word and melts them;
he stirs up his breezes, and the waters flow.

PSALM 147:8, 16, 18

AS YOU PRAISE GOD TODAY

- Reread the verses above, and praise God for overseeing the natural forces of our earth, such as the winds and rain.

THE FATHER SENT
THE SON

*Jesus said, "Just as the living Father sent me and
I live because of the Father, so the one who feeds
on me will live because of me."*

JOHN 6:57

*Jesus said, "I am one who testifies for myself;
my other witness is the Father, who sent me."*

JOHN 8:18

*We have seen and testify that the Father has sent
his Son to be the Savior of the world.*

1 JOHN 4:14

AS YOU PRAISE GOD TODAY

- Rejoice that God was willing to send his only
  Son from heaven to earth to die for you.

JESUS IS THE LAST ADAM

So it is written: "The first man Adam became a living being"; the last Adam, a life-giving spirit.
1 CORINTHIANS 15:45

The first Adam had a natural body of the dust of the ground and through him a natural body was given to his descendents. The last Adam, Christ, is the life-giving spirit who through his death and resurrection will at the second coming give his redeemed people a spiritual body—physical, yet imperishable, without corruption, and adaptable to live with God forever.

REFLECTING GOD STUDY BIBLE

AS YOU PRAISE GOD TODAY

- Praise God that just as we share in the fruit of the first Adam's sin, so will we share in the fruit of the last Adam's sacrifice, Jesus' death on the cross, which is eternal life.
- Rejoice that someday you will receive a spiritual body—physical, yet imperishable.

GOD OUR SAVIOR

Praise be to the LORD, to God our Savior,
who daily bears our burdens.

PSALM 68:19

At his appointed season God brought his word to
light through the preaching entrusted to me by
the command of God our Savior.

TITUS 1:3

When the kindness and love of God our Savior
appeared, he saved us, not because of righteous
things we had done, but because of his mercy.

TITUS 3:4–5

To the only God our Savior be glory, majesty,
power and authority, through Jesus Christ our
Lord, before all ages, now and forevermore! Amen.

JUDE 25

AS YOU PRAISE GOD TODAY

- Praise God for saving you—not because of the righteous things you have done, but because of his mercy.
- Thank him for daily bearing your burdens.

JESUS IS THE CONSOLATION OF ISRAEL

Now there was a man in Jerusalem called Simeon, who was righteous and devout. He was waiting for the consolation of Israel, and the Holy Spirit was upon him. It had been revealed to him by the Holy Spirit that he would not die before he had seen the Lord's Christ. Moved by the Spirit, he went into the temple courts. When the parents brought in the child Jesus to do for him what the custom of the Law required, Simeon took him in his arms and praised God, saying:
"Sovereign Lord, as you have promised, you now dismiss your servant in peace. For my eyes have seen your salvation, which you have prepared in the sight of all people, a light for revelation to the Gentiles and for glory to your people Israel."

LUKE 2:25–32

AS YOU PRAISE GOD TODAY

- Rejoice, for like Simeon, you will also see Jesus —either when he returns or in heaven.

JESUS WAS A CHILD

The LORD himself will give you a sign: The virgin will be with child and will give birth to a son, and will call him Immanuel.

ISAIAH 7:14

On coming to the house, the Magi saw the child with his mother Mary, and they bowed down and worshiped him. Then they opened their treasures and presented him with gifts of gold and of incense and of myrrh.

MATTHEW 2:11

Jesus grew in wisdom and stature, and in favor with God and men.

LUKE 2:52

AS YOU PRAISE GOD TODAY

- As the Magi did, worship Jesus and give him the treasure of your heart.
- Praise God for fulfilling his prophecy that the virgin would be with child and give birth to your Savior.

THE HOLY SPIRIT IS A GIFT

*Repent and be baptized, every one of you,
in the name of Jesus Christ for the forgiveness
of your sins. And you will receive
the gift of the Holy Spirit.*

ACTS 2:38

The gift of the Holy Spirit closes the gap between the life of God and ours. When we allow the love of God to move in us, we can no longer distinguish ours and his; he becomes us, he lives in us. It is the first fruits of the Spirit, the beginning of our being made divine.

AUSTIN FARRER

AS YOU PRAISE GOD TODAY

- Rejoice and give God thanks for the priceless gift of the Holy Spirit.
- Consider the fact that he chose to call the Holy Spirit a gift. Praise God for the ways in which the Spirit has been a gift to you.

JESUS IS THE IMAGE OF THE INVISIBLE GOD

*The Son is the image of the invisible God, the
firstborn over all creation.*

COLOSSIANS 1:15

*The Son is the radiance of God's glory and the
exact representation of his being.*

HEBREWS 1:3

*Your attitude should be the same
as that of Christ Jesus:
Who, being in very nature God,
did not consider equality with God something
to be grasped,
but made himself nothing,
taking the very nature of a servant,
being made in human likeness.*

PHILIPPIANS 2:5–7

AS YOU PRAISE GOD TODAY

- Rejoice that God, who is beyond your comprehension, chose to reveal himself to you in the form of Jesus Christ.

JESUS IS THE FOUNTAIN

Jesus said, "Whoever believes in me, as the
Scripture has said, streams of living water will
flow from within him."
JOHN 7:38

With you is the fountain of life;
in your light we see light, O LORD.
PSALM 36:9

A fountain will flow out of the LORD's house.
JOEL 3:18

Fountain of life, and all-abounding grace,
Our source, our center, and our dwelling place!
MADAME JEANNE MARIE DE LA MOTHE GUYON

AS YOU PRAISE GOD TODAY

- Rejoice that Jesus is a fountain that will never run dry.
- Thank Jesus for being the source of living water for you.

GOD FORGIVES

ELOHAY SELICHOT

*Praise the LORD, O my soul,
and forget not all his benefits—
who forgives all your sins.*
PSALM 103:2–3

When we confess our failings to God, he willingly offers us forgiveness. We can count on it. He will not refuse to forgive even if we make another mistake. Yet there may be times when we don't *feel* forgiven, times when we feel we've crossed an invisible line, and God will give up on us. The Bible reassures us that though our feelings are fleeting, God's forgiveness is constant. If we confess our sins, he *will* forgive us. It's a promise we can bank on. And it's a promise we can share with others, too.

SARAH M. HUPP

AS YOU PRAISE GOD TODAY

- Thank God for his willingness to forgive you when you are truly sorry, no matter what you have done.
- Praise him that even when you don't feel forgiven, you can rely on God's promise that you are.

THE HOLY SPIRIT IS YOUR TEACHER

[Jesus told his disciples], "When you are brought before synagogues, rulers and authorities, do not worry about how you will defend yourselves or what you will say, for the Holy Spirit will teach you at that time what you should say."

LUKE 12:11–12

Without the present illumination of the Holy Spirit, the Word of God must remain a dead letter to every man, no matter how intelligent or well-educated he may be. . . . It is just as essential for the Holy Spirit to reveal the truth of Scripture to the reader today as it was necessary for him to inspire the writers in their day.

WILLIAM LAW

AS YOU PRAISE GOD TODAY

- Praise God for the wonderful blessing of the Holy Spirit, who is your teacher.
- Thank him for illuminating God's Word for you and revealing the treasures it holds.

GOD'S NAME IS GLORIOUS

Now, our God, we give you thanks,
and praise your glorious name.
1 CHRONICLES 29:13

Stand up and praise the LORD your God,
who is from everlasting to everlasting.
Blessed be your glorious name, and may it
be exalted above all blessing and praise.
NEHEMIAH 9:5

Praise be to his glorious name forever;
may the whole earth be filled with his glory.
Amen and Amen.
PSALM 72:19

I will praise you, O LORD my God,
with all my heart;
I will glorify your name forever.
PSALM 86:12

AS YOU PRAISE GOD TODAY

- Praise God for making such a glorious name for himself.
- Thank him for all his marvelous miracles.
- Exalt his glorious name by giving God praise.

JESUS IS THE HEAD OF ALL THINGS

Now I want you to realize that the head of every man is Christ, and the head of the woman is man, and the head of Christ is God.

1 CORINTHIANS 11:3

God made known to us the mystery of his will ... to be put into effect when the times will have reached their fulfillment—to bring all things in heaven and on earth together under one head, even Christ.

EPHESIANS 1:9–10

You have been given fullness in Christ, who is the head over every power and authority.

COLOSSIANS 2:10

AS YOU PRAISE GOD TODAY

- Rejoice that God has made Jesus the head of all things, and exalted Jesus above all others.
- Think about the divine order God established in making Jesus the head of all things and how it affects your life. Praise him as you realize both the benefits and the responsibilities.

THE HOLY ONE
OF ISRAEL

<u>KADOSH</u>

*Shout aloud and sing for joy, people of Zion,
for great is the Holy One of Israel among you.*

ISAIAH 12:6

*"Fear not, for I have redeemed you;
I have summoned you by name; you are mine.
When you pass through the waters,
I will be with you;
and when you pass through the rivers,
they will not sweep over you.
When you walk through the fire,
you will not be burned;
the flames will not set you ablaze.
For I am the LORD, your God,
the Holy One of Israel, your Savior."*

ISAIAH 43:1–3

<u>AS YOU PRAISE GOD TODAY</u>

- Rejoice that the Holy One of Israel took it upon himself to make you holy, so you could be in right relationship with him.

THE NAME OF JESUS IS ABOVE EVERY NAME

*God exalted Jesus Christ to the highest place
and gave him the name that is above every name,
that at the name of Jesus every knee should bow,
in heaven and on earth and under the earth,
and every tongue confess that Jesus Christ is Lord,
to the glory of God the Father.*

PHILIPPIANS 2:9–11

AS YOU PRAISE GOD TODAY

- Praise God for giving Jesus the name that is above all names.
- Praise him for the power that is manifested when the name of Jesus is spoken.

JESUS IS YOUR ATONEMENT

All have sinned and fall short of the glory of God, and are justified freely by his grace through the redemption that came by Christ Jesus. God presented him as a sacrifice of atonement, through faith in his blood.

ROMANS 3:23–25

Jesus Christ is the atoning sacrifice for our sins, and not only for ours but also for the sins of the whole world.

1 JOHN 2:2

This is love: not that we loved God, but that he loved us and sent his Son as an atoning sacrifice for our sins.

1 JOHN 4:10

AS YOU PRAISE GOD TODAY

- Praise him for presenting Jesus as an atoning sacrifice for you.
- Think about Hebrews 2:17. Jesus went through all the pain and difficulty of a human life so he could fully understand our needs. Praise him for that!

JESUS IS THE FIRSTBORN OF THE FATHER

Christ is the image of the invisible God, the firstborn over all creation. For by him all things were created: . . . all things were created by him and for him. He is before all things.

COLOSSIANS 1:15–17

When God brings his firstborn into the world, he says, "Let all God's angels worship him."

HEBREWS 1:6

The Lord said, "He will call out to me, 'You are my Father, my God, the Rock my Savior.' I will also appoint him my firstborn, the most exalted of the kings of the earth."

PSALM 89:26–27

AS YOU PRAISE GOD TODAY

- Exalt Jesus above all others. Just as the firstborn son of an earthly father has certain rights and privileges, Jesus, as firstborn of the Father, has preeminence over all creation and all created beings.
- Praise God for his willingness to offer his firstborn Son as a sacrifice to gain you as his child.

GOD IS THE SUSTAINER OF THE UNIVERSE

He is before all things,
and in him all things hold together.
COLOSSIANS 1:17

Praise the LORD, O my soul.
O LORD my God, you are very great. . . .
He set the earth on its foundations;
it can never be moved. . . .
The moon marks off the seasons,
and the sun knows when to go down. . . .
May the glory of the LORD endure forever;
may the LORD rejoice in his works.
PSALM 104:1, 5, 19, 31

The Son is the radiance of God's glory and the
exact representation of his being, sustaining all
things by his powerful word.
HEBREWS 1:3

AS YOU PRAISE GOD TODAY

• Praise God for the order of his universe, an order held together by Jesus.

JESUS IS THE HEAD OF THE CHURCH

*The Son is the head of the body, the church;
he is the beginning and the firstborn from
among the dead, so that in everything
he might have the supremacy.*

COLOSSIANS 1:18

*The husband is the head of the wife as Christ is
the head of the church, his body, of which
he is the Savior.*

EPHESIANS 5:23

*Speaking the truth in love, we will in all things
grow up into him who is the Head, that is, Christ.*

EPHESIANS 4:15

AS YOU PRAISE GOD TODAY

- Worship Jesus as the head of his body, the Church.
- Praise the Father for appointing Jesus as the head of the Church.

JESUS IS THE FIRSTBORN FROM THE DEAD

Grace and peace to you from Jesus Christ, who is the faithful witness, the firstborn from the dead, and the ruler of the kings of the earth.

REVELATION 1:4–5

Christ has indeed been raised from the dead, the firstfruits of those who have fallen asleep. For since death came through a man, the resurrection of the dead comes also through a man.

1 CORINTHIANS 15:20–21

AS YOU PRAISE GOD TODAY

- Rejoice that just as death had no power over Jesus, death will have no power over you.
- Rejoice that because Jesus was the firstborn from the dead, you are one of his many brothers and sisters when you accept him as your resurrected Lord and Savior.

THE SPIRIT OF SONSHIP

*Those who are led by the Spirit of God are sons of
God. For you did not receive a spirit that makes
you a slave again to fear, but you received the
Spirit of sonship. And by him we cry, "Abba,
Father." The Spirit himself testifies with our
spirit that we are God's children.*

ROMANS 8:14–16

*Because you are sons, God sent the Spirit of his
Son into our hearts, the Spirit who calls out,
"Abba, Father."*

GALATIANS 4:6

A man adopts one for his son and heir that does
not at all resemble him; but whosoever God
adopts for His child is like Him; he not only bears
His heavenly Father's name, but His image.

THOMAS WATSON

AS YOU PRAISE GOD TODAY

- Rejoice that God chose to make you his child.
  He adopted you because he wants you to be his
  son! Some Bibles translate the term "Spirit of
  sonship" as the "Spirit of adoption."
- Rejoice that not only is Jesus God's Son, you are
  God's child, too.

JESUS IS THE MYSTERY OF GOD

To [his saints] God has chosen to make known among the Gentiles the glorious riches of this mystery, which is Christ in you, the hope of glory.
COLOSSIANS 1:27

My purpose is that they may be encouraged in heart and united in love, so that they may have the full riches of complete understanding, in order that they may know the mystery of God, namely, Christ.
COLOSSIANS 2:2

God made known to us the mystery of his will according to his good pleasure, which he purposed in Christ, to be put into effect when the times will have reached their fulfillment—to bring all things in heaven and on earth together under one head, even Christ.
EPHESIANS 1:9–10

AS YOU PRAISE GOD TODAY

- Praise God for revealing the mystery to you, so you can experience for yourself what it is like to have Jesus dwelling in you, the hope of glory.
- Praise him for his amazing plan to reveal the Messiah to the Gentiles as well as the Jews.

GOD IS INVISIBLE

Now to the King eternal, immortal, invisible,
the only God, be honor and glory
for ever and ever. Amen.
1 TIMOTHY 1:17

No one has ever seen God,
but God the One and Only, who is at
the Father's side, has made him known.
JOHN 1:18

No one has ever seen God; but if we love
one another, God lives in us and his love
is made complete in us.
1 JOHN 4:12

AS YOU PRAISE GOD TODAY

- Honor God by praising him even though you do not see him with your physical eyes.
- Praise God for revealing himself to you, so you can see him with the eye of faith.

JESUS IS YOUR MEDIATOR

*There is one God and one mediator between
God and men, the man Christ Jesus.*
1 TIMOTHY 2:5

*Christ is the mediator of a new covenant,
that those who are called may receive
the promised eternal inheritance.*
HEBREWS 9:15

*You have come to God, the judge of all men,
to the spirits of righteous men made perfect,
to Jesus the mediator of a new covenant.*
HEBREWS 12:23–24

AS YOU PRAISE GOD TODAY

- Thank Jesus for acting as your mediator, reconciling you to the Father.
- Thank the Father for sending his Son to earth to mediate between himself and you.

JESUS IS THE SON OF MARY

An angel of the Lord appeared to Joseph in a dream and said, "Joseph son of David, do not be afraid to take Mary home as your wife, because what is conceived in her is from the Holy Spirit. She will give birth to a son, and you are to give him the name Jesus, because he will save his people from their sins."

MATTHEW 1:20–21

Jesus began to teach in the synagogue, and many who heard him were amazed.
"Where did this man get these things?" they asked. "What's this wisdom that has been given him, that he even does miracles! Isn't this the carpenter? Isn't this Mary's son?"

MARK 6:2–3

AS YOU PRAISE GOD TODAY

- Praise him for his amazing plan to send his own son to be born of a woman.
- Think about what it must have been like for both Mary and Jesus to share their unique relationship. Give God thanks for his flawless plan.

GOD CONTROLS THE SEASONS

God has shown kindness by giving you rain from heaven and crops in their seasons.
ACTS 14:17

God said, "Let there be lights in the expanse of the sky to separate the day from the night, and let them serve as signs to mark seasons and days and years."
GENESIS 1:14

God changes times and seasons.
DANIEL 2:21

AS YOU PRAISE GOD TODAY

- Give God your praise for overseeing all the seasons and keeping their timing perfect.
- Praise him for the variety among the different seasons, rejoicing over the good things each season brings.

THE FATHER LISTENS TO THE SON

Jesus looked up and said, "Father, I thank you that you have heard me. I knew that you always hear me, but I said this for the benefit of the people standing here, that they may believe that you sent me."
JOHN 11:41–42

Jesus said, "Father, glorify your name!"
Then a voice came from heaven, "I have glorified it, and will glorify it again."
JOHN 12:28

AS YOU PRAISE GOD TODAY

- Give God praise for hearing his Son Jesus when he calls. Rejoice because God hears you, too!
- Praise Jesus and his Father for the example they set by demonstrating their own special relationship for you and those you love.

JESUS IS THE HEIR OF ALL THINGS

*In these last days God has spoken to us by his Son,
whom he appointed heir of all things, and
through whom he made the universe.*

HEBREWS 1:2

*I will proclaim the decree of the LORD:
He said to me, "You are my Son;
today I have become your Father.
Ask of me,
and I will make the nations your inheritance,
the ends of the earth your possession."*

PSALM 2:7–8

AS YOU PRAISE GOD TODAY

- Praise Jesus as the one to whom all things belong.
  Remember that everything belongs to Jesus, and
  that everything includes you.
- Praise the Father for giving Jesus the nations as
  his inheritance.
- Praise the holy name of Jesus. He inherited a
  name that is superior to that of the angels.

GOD IS MAJESTIC

God, you are resplendent with light,
more majestic than mountains rich with game.
PSALM 76:4

The LORD reigns, he is robed in majesty.
PSALM 93:1

Who among the gods is like you, O LORD?
Who is like you—
majestic in holiness,
awesome in glory,
working wonders?
EXODUS 15:11

AS YOU PRAISE GOD TODAY

- Give God praise and magnify him as you reflect on him in all his majestic glory.
- Praise him as you ponder what heaven will be like when all the saints join together to worship God in all his majesty.

GOD MAKES ROUGH PLACES SMOOTH

A voice of one calling:
"In the desert prepare
the way for the LORD;
make straight in the wilderness
a highway for our God.
Every valley shall be raised up,
every mountain and hill made low;
the rough ground shall become level,
the rugged places a plain.
And the glory of the LORD will be revealed,
and all mankind together will see it.
For the mouth of the LORD has spoken."

ISAIAH 40:3–5

AS YOU PRAISE GOD TODAY

- Rejoice! If the road you are traveling is rough and difficult, God will make it smooth.
- Thank God for helping you not to stumble.

JESUS IS LIKE THE SUN

... because of the tender mercy of our God,
by which the rising sun will come
to us from heaven
to shine on those living in darkness
and in the shadow of death,
to guide our feet into the path of peace.
LUKE 1:78–79

Our great High Priest is in glory, exalted above all created angels. But he is the same Jesus we knew in the days of his flesh. He is the same Jesus in heaven as he was on earth, as he was before the world began. The face shining above the brightness of the sun is the face that drew sinners to his feet. The hand that holds the seven stars is the hand that was laid in blessing upon little children. The breast girt about with a golden girdle is the breast upon which the beloved disciple laid his head at the last supper.

A. D. FOREMAN, JR.

AS YOU PRAISE GOD TODAY

- Give Jesus praise by saying, "All glory belongs to you, Lord Jesus. Be exalted in your glory!" Jesus is so full of glory that the sun is the only thing in our world that could be remotely similar in comparison.

JESUS IS THE GREAT HIGH PRIEST

Since we have a great high priest who has gone through the heavens, Jesus the Son of God, let us hold firmly to the faith we profess. For we do not have a high priest who is unable to sympathize with our weaknesses, but we have one who has been tempted in every way, just as we are—yet was without sin.

HEBREWS 4:14–15

Because Jesus lives forever, he has a permanent priesthood. Therefore he is able to save completely those who come to God through him, because he always lives to intercede for them. Such a high priest meets our need—one who is holy, blameless, pure, set apart from sinners, exalted above the heavens. Unlike the other high priests, Jesus does not need to offer sacrifices day after day, first for his own sins, and then for the sins of the people. He sacrificed for their sins once for all when he offered himself.

HEBREWS 7:24–27

AS YOU PRAISE GOD TODAY

- Thank Jesus for being the perfect high priest, who once and for all, sacrificed himself for your sins.

JESUS IS THE SON OF JOSEPH

All spoke well of Jesus and were amazed at the gracious words that came from his lips. "Isn't this Joseph's son?" they asked.

LUKE 4:22

Now Jesus himself was about thirty years old when he began his ministry. He was the son, so it was thought, of Joseph.

LUKE 3:23

Philip found Nathanael and told him, "We have found the one Moses wrote about in the Law, and about whom the prophets also wrote— Jesus of Nazareth, the son of Joseph."

JOHN 1:45

AS YOU PRAISE GOD TODAY

- Read Matthew 1:19–25, and 2:13–15. Praise God for the faithfulness and obedience of Joseph in the life of Jesus.

THE FATHER EXALTS HIS SON

*Jesus, who, being in very nature God,
did not consider equality with God
something to be grasped,
but made himself nothing,
taking the very nature of a servant,
being made in human likeness.
And being found in appearance as a man,
he humbled himself
and became obedient to death—
even death on a cross!
Therefore God exalted him to the highest place
and gave him the name that is above every name,
that at the name of Jesus every knee should bow,
in heaven and on earth and under the earth,
and every tongue confess that Jesus Christ is Lord,
to the glory of God the Father.*

PHILIPPIANS 2:6–11

AS YOU PRAISE GOD TODAY

- Give Jesus honor, glory and praise as the exalted
  One of the Father.
- Praise God for exalting his Son to the highest
  place of all.

GOD INSPIRED THE WRITING OF SCRIPTURE

The Spirit of the LORD spoke through me;
his word was on my tongue.

2 SAMUEL 23:2

"As for me, this is my covenant with them," says the
LORD. "My Spirit, who is on you, and my words
that I have put in your mouth will not depart from
your mouth, or from the mouths of your children,
or from the mouths of their descendants from this
time on and forever," says the LORD.

ISAIAH 59:21

All Scripture is God-breathed and is useful for
teaching, rebuking, correcting and training in
righteousness, so that the man of God may be
thoroughly equipped for every good work.

2 TIMOTHY 3:16–17

AS YOU PRAISE GOD TODAY

- Thank God for the many ways you can benefit from his Word, the Bible.
- Take time to consider how amazing the Bible is. Its books were written by so many different men, yet every word is God-breathed. Worship God as you reflect on this miracle.

JESUS IS THE AUTHOR OF LIFE, SALVATION, AND FAITH

[The Apostle Peter said to people at Solomon's Colonnade,] "You killed the author of life, but God raise him from the dead."

ACTS 3:15

In bringing many sons to glory, it was fitting that God, for whom and through whom everything exists, should make the author of their salvation perfect through suffering.

HEBREWS 2:10

Let us fix our eyes on Jesus, the author and perfecter of our faith, who for the joy set before him endured the cross, scorning its shame, and sat down at the right hand of the throne of God.

HEBREWS 12:2

AS YOU PRAISE GOD TODAY

- Rejoice that Jesus is the author of your life, salvation and faith. Give him glory and praise.
- Anything Jesus authors is a success in the end. Praise him for seeing everything he authors through to its conclusion.

JESUS CAME AS A BABY

*While [Mary and Joseph were in Bethlehem], the
time came for the baby to be born, and she gave
birth to her firstborn, a son. She wrapped him in
cloths and placed him in a manger, because there
was no room for them in the inn.*

LUKE 2:6–7

*The angel said [to the shepherds], "Do not be
afraid. I bring you good news of great joy that will
be for all the people. Today in the town of David a
Savior has been born to you; he is Christ the Lord.
This will be a sign to you: You will find a baby
wrapped in cloths and lying in a manger."... So
they hurried off and found Mary and Joseph, and
the baby, who was lying in the manger.*

LUKE 2:10–12, 16

*For lo! the world's great Shepherd now is born,
A blessed babe, an infant full of power.*

EDMUND BOLTON

AS YOU PRAISE GOD TODAY

- Rejoice! Meditate on the fact that the One who
  created the universe brought to earth an inno-
  cent child to be a sacrifice for you. Because of
  him, you live!

GOD IS A CONSUMING FIRE

*Since we are receiving a kingdom that cannot be
shaken, let us be thankful, and so worship God
acceptably with reverence and awe, for our "God
is a consuming fire."*
HEBREWS 12:28–29

*See, the Name of the LORD comes from afar, ...
and his tongue is a consuming fire.*
ISAIAH 30:27

Eternal Trinity ... you are a fire, ever burning and
never consumed. You consume in your heart all
the self-love within my soul, taking away all cold-
ness. You are a light, ever shining and never fading.
You drive away all the darkness within my heart,
enabling me to see your glorious truth.

CATHERINE OF SIENA

AS YOU PRAISE GOD TODAY

- Reflect on the fact that he is a fire that destroys
  and purifies but also warms your heart and soul.
- Worship God as you allow yourself to be
  consumed with and by him. Worship him with
  your whole spirit, soul, and body.

GOD IS YOUR TEACHER

This is what the LORD says—
your Redeemer, the Holy One of Israel:
"I am the LORD your God,
who teaches you what is best for you."
ISAIAH 48:17

"Do men make their own gods?
Yes, but they are not gods!
Therefore I will teach them—
this time I will teach them
my power and might.
Then they will know
that my name is the LORD."
JEREMIAH 16:20–21

Come, let us go up to the mountain of the LORD,
to the house of the God of Jacob.
He will teach us his ways,
so that we may walk in his paths.
MICAH 4:2

AS YOU PRAISE GOD TODAY

- Thank God for being a Teacher to you.
- Praise him for teaching you about his power and might, his ways, and what is best for you. God is the Teacher above all teachers. Hallelujah!

GOD IS A GIVER OF GIFTS

Every good and perfect gift is from above, coming down from the Father of the heavenly lights, who does not change like shifting shadows.

JAMES 1:17

The wages of sin is death, but the gift of God is eternal life in Christ Jesus our Lord.

ROMANS 6:23

Whoever is thirsty, let him come; and whoever wishes, let him take the free gift of the water of life.

REVELATION 22:17

AS YOU PRAISE GOD TODAY

- Think of all the good and perfect gifts God has given you, and praise him for his generosity.
- Praise God for the gifts of righteousness, eternal life, and the water of life.

GOD IS THE LAWGIVER

The LORD is our judge,
the LORD is our lawgiver,
the LORD is our king;
it is he who will save us.
ISAIAH 33:22

There is only one Lawgiver and Judge,
the one who is able to save and destroy.
JAMES 4:12

The law was put in charge to lead us to Christ
that we might be justified by faith.
GALATIANS 3:24

AS YOU PRAISE GOD TODAY

• Read Exodus 32:16. Give God praise as you
  think about him engraving his laws into stone.
• Praise God for giving the law to lead us to
  Christ.

GOD DISCIPLINES US

Blessed is the man you discipline, O LORD,
the man you teach from your law.
PSALM 94:12

Do not despise the LORD's discipline
and do not resent his rebuke,
because the LORD disciplines those he loves,
as a father the son he delights in.
PROVERBS 3:11–12

God disciplines us for our good, that we may
share in his holiness. No discipline seems pleasant
at the time, but painful. Later on, however, it
produces a harvest of righteousness and peace for
those who have been trained by it.
HEBREWS 12:10–11

AS YOU PRAISE GOD TODAY

- Praise God for disciplining you, because it means he loves you and accepts you as his child.
- Thank God for allowing you to share in his holiness through his discipline.
- Rejoice in the harvest of righteousness and peace that is produced in your life.

GOD KEEPS YOU

Jesus said, "My sheep listen to my voice; I know them, and they follow me. I give them eternal life, and they shall never perish; no one can snatch them out of my hand. My Father, who has given them to me, is greater than all; no one can snatch them out of my Father's hand."

JOHN 10:27–29

Jesus said, "I will remain in the world no longer, but [my followers] are still in the world, and I am coming to you. Holy Father, protect them by the power of your name—the name you gave me —so that they may be one as we are one. While I was with them, I protected them and kept them safe by that name you gave me. . . . My prayer is not that you take them out of the world but that you protect them from the evil one."

JOHN 17: 11–12, 15

AS YOU PRAISE GOD TODAY

- Praise Jesus for praying to the Father for you.
- Rejoice that you are safe in the Father's hands.

JESUS IS THE SON OF ABRAHAM

God said to Abram, "As for me, this is my covenant with you: You will be the father of many nations. No longer will you be called Abram; your name will be Abraham, for I have made you a father of many nations. I will make you very fruitful; I will make nations of you, and kings will come from you. I will establish my covenant as an everlasting covenant between me and you and your descendants after you."

GENESIS 17:3–7

God redeemed us in order that the blessing given to Abraham might come to the Gentiles through Christ Jesus . . . The promises were spoken to Abraham and to his seed. The Scripture does not say "and to seeds," meaning many people, but "and to your seed," meaning one person, who is Christ.

GALATIANS 3:14, 16

AS YOU PRAISE GOD TODAY

- Praise God for keeping the covenant promise he made to Abraham.
- Praise him for allowing you to share in the covenant through Jesus.

THE FATHER PREDESTINES BELIEVERS

*Those God foreknew he also predestined
to be conformed to the likeness of his Son,
that he might be the firstborn among
many brothers. And those he predestined,
he also called; those he called, he also justified;
those he justified, he also glorified.*

ROMANS 8:29–30

*God predestined us to be adopted as his sons
through Jesus Christ, in accordance with his
pleasure and will. . . . In him we were also chosen,
having been predestined according to the plan of
him who works out everything in conformity
with the purpose of his will.*

EPHESIANS 1:5, 11

*He chose to give us birth through
the word of truth.*

JAMES 1:18

AS YOU PRAISE GOD TODAY

- Read Acts 2:21 and praise God that he saves you.
- Thank God for predestining, calling, justifying, and glorifying you.

LORD

ADONAI

*[David] said to the LORD, "You are my Lord;
apart from you I have no good thing."*
PSALM 16:2

*The other disciples told [Thomas], "We have seen
the Lord!"*
*But he said to them, "Unless I see the nail marks
in his hands and put my finger where the nails
were, and put my hand into his side, I will not
believe it."*
*A week later Jesus' disciples were in the house
again, and Thomas was with them. Though the
doors were locked, Jesus came and stood among
them and said, "Peace be with you!" Then he
said to Thomas, "Put your finger here; see my
hands. Reach out your hand and put it into my
side. Stop doubting and believe."*
Thomas said to him, "My Lord and my God!"
JOHN 20:25–28

AS YOU PRAISE GOD TODAY

- Think about one way that God is your Lord.
  Rejoice that he is a loving Lord.

GOD IS SOVEREIGN

Our God is a God who saves;
from the Sovereign LORD comes escape from death.
PSALM 68:20

As the soil makes the sprout come up
and a garden causes seeds to grow,
so the Sovereign LORD will make
righteousness and praise
spring up before all nations.
ISAIAH 61:11

The LORD Almighty will swallow up death forever.
The Sovereign LORD will wipe away the tears
from all faces;
he will remove the disgrace of his people
from all the earth.
The LORD has spoken.
ISAIAH 25:8

AS YOU PRAISE GOD TODAY

- Rejoice that the Sovereign Lord, the supreme ruler of all, is your Lord.
- Praise him that his purpose will stand. God will have his way, no matter what.

JESUS IS THE BREAD OF LIFE

Jesus declared, "I am the bread of life. He who comes to me will never go hungry, and he who believes in me will never be thirsty."

JOHN 6:35

Jesus understands the deep longings of the human heart. He made us with needs for intimacy that only he could meet. Many of us attempt to meet these needs through substitutes like sex, money, or work. But ultimately only Jesus can satisfy.

He is the bread of life. Good bread nourishes and strengthens our bodies. The substitutes we use are like candy. They may taste sweet, but they never really satisfy our hunger.

CHRISTIAN GROWTH STUDY BIBLE

AS YOU PRAISE GOD TODAY

- Praise him for Jesus, the bread that takes away all your hunger forever.
- Think of all the ways Jesus has satisfied your needs over the years. Thank him and praise him for what he has done and will do.

JESUS IS THE FAITHFUL WITNESS

Grace and peace to you from . . . Jesus Christ,
who is the faithful witness, the firstborn from the
dead, and the ruler of the kings of the earth.

REVELATION 1:4–5

L ord Jesus, You are the faithful Witness—our
 witness to God and God's witness to us.

NIV WORSHIP BIBLE

AS YOU PRAISE GOD TODAY

- Praise Jesus for revealing to you who God really is, and praise the Father for sending Jesus to make himself known.
- Ask God to fill you with the Holy Spirit so that you, too, can become a faithful witness to God's truth.

ALPHA AND THE OMEGA

"I am the Alpha and the Omega,"
says the Lord God, "who is, and who was,
and who is to come, the Almighty."
REVELATION 1:8

Jesus said, "I am the Alpha and the Omega, the
First and the Last, the Beginning and the End."
REVELATION 22:13

J esus Christ states that he is the "first and the last,"
the same designation God had given himself in
the Book of Isaiah (Isaiah 44:6; 48:12). This description reinforces Christ's equality with the Father as a
member of the Trinity. Christ lives outside the
confines of time, having neither beginning nor end.
LIFE PROMISES BIBLE

AS YOU PRAISE GOD TODAY

- Consider that Alpha and Omega are the first
  and last letters of the Greek alphabet just as Jesus
  is the first and the last of all. Worship Jesus as
  you realize the wonder of his having no beginning or end. He was, and is, and is to come.
- Reflect on the fact that Jesus is your uncreated
  Creator.

GOD HEARS

Evening, morning and noon
I cry out in distress,
and God hears my voice.
PSALM 55:17

The LORD hears the needy
and does not despise his captive people.
PSALM 69:33

The LORD fulfills the desires of those who fear him;
he hears their cry and saves them.
PSALM 145:19

AS YOU PRAISE GOD TODAY

- Praise God! He hears you when you call.
- Even if no one seems to have time for you, rejoice because God's ear is always open to listen.

GOD IS PLEASED WITH JESUS

As soon as Jesus was baptized, he went up out of the water. At that moment heaven was opened, and he saw the Spirit of God descending like a dove and lighting on him. And a voice from heaven said, "This is my Son, whom I love; with him I am well pleased."

MATTHEW 3:16–17

Jesus took with him Peter, James and John the brother of James, and led them up a high mountain by themselves. There he was transfigured before them. . . . A bright cloud enveloped them, and a voice from the cloud said, "This is my Son, whom I love; with him I am well pleased. Listen to him!"

MATTHEW 17:1–2, 5

AS YOU PRAISE GOD TODAY

• Praise God for showering his Son with his approval. Think about how much it means to you when you know your parents are pleased with you.

THE HOLY SPIRIT GIVES YOU A FRUITFUL LIFE

The fruit of the Spirit is love, joy, peace,
patience, kindness, goodness, faithfulness,
gentleness and self-control.
GALATIANS 5:22–23

Jesus said, "Remain in me, and I will remain
in you. No branch can bear fruit by itself;
it must remain in the vine. Neither can you
bear fruit unless you remain in me. I am the
vine; you are the branches. If a man remains
in me and I in him, he will bear much fruit;
apart from me you can do nothing."
JOHN 15:4–5

This is my prayer: that you may be able to discern
what is best and may be pure and blameless until
the day of Christ, filled with the fruit of
righteousness that comes through Jesus Christ—
to the glory and praise of God.
PHILIPPIANS 1:9–11

AS YOU PRAISE GOD TODAY

- Thank God for the fruit of the Spirit and that you can partake of it.
- Thank Jesus that you are connected to him, and as you remain in him you will bear fruit.

GOD IS TRIUMPHANT

"Do not weep! See, the Lion of the tribe of Judah,
the Root of David, has triumphed."
REVELATION 5:5

The LORD will march out like a mighty man,
like a warrior he will stir up his zeal;
with a shout he will raise the battle cry
and will triumph over his enemies.
ISAIAH 42:13

Thanks be to God, who always leads us in
triumphal procession in Christ and through
us spreads everywhere the fragrance of the
knowledge of him.
2 CORINTHIANS 2:14

AS YOU PRAISE GOD TODAY

- Give praise to God because he always leads you
  in triumphal procession in Christ.
- Worship Jesus as the glorious Lion of the Tribe
  of Judah who triumphs over all.

JESUS CASTS OUT DEMONS

When evening came, many who were demon-possessed were brought to Jesus, and he drove out the spirits with a word.

MATTHEW 8:16

In the synagogue there was a man possessed by a demon, an evil spirit. He cried out at the top of his voice, "Ha! What do you want with us, Jesus of Nazareth? Have you come to destroy us? I know who you are—the Holy One of God!"
"Be quiet!" Jesus said sternly. "Come out of him!"
Then the demon threw the man down before them all and came out without injuring him.

LUKE 4:33–35

AS YOU PRAISE GOD TODAY

• Rejoice that Jesus has dominion over demons. No demonic power can stand against him!

JESUS IS THE BRANCH

*The Branch of the LORD will be beautiful and
glorious, and the fruit of the land will be the
pride and glory of the survivors in Israel.*

ISAIAH 4:2

*A shoot will come up from the stump of Jesse;
from his roots a Branch will bear fruit.*

ISAIAH 11:1

*"The days are coming," declares the LORD,
"when I will raise up to David
a righteous Branch,
a King who will reign wisely
and do what is just and right in the land."*

JEREMIAH 23:5

AS YOU PRAISE GOD TODAY

- Praise Jesus as the Branch, the One the Lord said
  would be beautiful and glorious.
- Rejoice because the Branch bears fruit and does
  what is just and right.

THE FATHER AND THE SON GLORIFY ONE ANOTHER

Jesus looked toward heaven and prayed:
"Father, the time has come. Glorify your Son,
that your Son may glorify you. For you granted
him authority over all people that he might give
eternal life to all those you have given him. Now
this is eternal life: that they may know you, the
only true God, and Jesus Christ, whom you have
sent. I have brought you glory on earth by
completing the work you gave me to do. And now,
Father, glorify me in your presence with the glory
I had with you before the world began.

JOHN 17:1–5

AS YOU PRAISE GOD TODAY

- The Father and the Son glorify one another. Now
  you glorify them by singing praises to them. Read
  Psalm 34:3, Psalm 63:3, and Psalm 86:12.

JESUS IS A MIRACLE-WORKER

A man named Lazarus was sick.
The sisters sent word to Jesus, "Lord, the one
you love is sick."
When he heard this, Jesus said, "This sickness will not
end in death. No, it is for God's glory so that God's
Son may be glorified through it."
Jesus said to her, "I am the resurrection and the life.
He who believes in me will live, even though he dies;
and whoever lives and believes in me will never die.
Do you believe this?"
"Yes, Lord," she told him, "I believe that you are
the Christ, the Son of God, who was
to come into the world."
Jesus, once more deeply moved, came to the tomb. Jesus
called in a loud voice, "Lazarus, come out!" The dead
man came out, his hands and feet wrapped with strips
of linen, and a cloth around his face. Jesus said to them,
"Take off the grave clothes and let him go."
Therefore many of the Jews who had come to visit Mary,
and had seen what Jesus did, put their faith in him.
JOHN 11:1, 3–6, 17–27, 38, 43–45

AS YOU PRAISE GOD TODAY

- Rejoice and praise Jesus for being a miracle-worker.

GOD HEALS THE BROKENHEARTED

The LORD is close to the brokenhearted
and saves those who are crushed in spirit.
PSALM 34:18

God heals the brokenhearted
and binds up their wounds.
PSALM 147:3

The Spirit of the Sovereign LORD is on me. . . .
He has sent me to bind up the brokenhearted.
ISAIAH 61:1

God does not leave us comfortless, but we have to be in dire need of comfort to know the truth of his promise. It is in time of calamity . . . in days and nights of sorrow and trouble that the presence, the sufficiency, and the sympathy of God grow very sure and very wonderful. Then we find out that the grace of God is sufficient for all our needs, for every problem, and for every difficulty, for every broken heart, and for every human sorrow.

PETER MARSHALL

AS YOU PRAISE GOD TODAY

- Praise God for being a compassionate Father who heals your heart when it is broken.

GOD CHOSE YOU

*God chose us in him before the creation of the
world to be holy and blameless in his sight.*

EPHESIANS 1:4

*We ought always to thank God for you, brothers
loved by the Lord, because from the beginning
God chose you to be saved through the sanctifying
work of the Spirit and through belief in the truth.*

2 THESSALONIANS 2:13

*You are a chosen people, a royal priesthood, a
holy nation, a people belonging to God, that you
may declare the praises of him who called you out
of darkness into his wonderful light.*

1 PETER 2:9

AS YOU PRAISE GOD TODAY

- Praise God—he chose you! Do you remember
  when you were a child and people were being
  picked for teams? Do you remember a feeling of
  fear, hoping you weren't the last one chosen? You
  never have to fear rejection with God—you are
  precious to him!

JESUS IS COMING SOON

In just a very little while,
"He who is coming will come and will
not delay."
HEBREWS 10:37

Be patient and stand firm, because the Lord's
coming is near.
JAMES 5:8

Jesus said, "Behold, I am coming soon! My
reward is with me, and I will give to everyone
according to what he has done."
REVELATION 22:12

Jesus who testifies to these things says,
"Yes, I am coming soon."
Amen. Come, Lord Jesus.
REVELATION 22:20

AS YOU PRAISE GOD TODAY

- Look forward with confident expectation for the soon-coming arrival of Jesus, and give him praise.

GOD OF YOUR PRAISE

ELOHAY TEHILATI

*Praise the LORD.
Praise God in his sanctuary;
praise him in his mighty heavens.
Praise him for his acts of power;
praise him for his surpassing greatness.
Praise him with the sounding of the trumpet,
praise him with the harp and lyre,
praise him with tambourine and dancing,
praise him with the strings and flute,
praise him with the clash of cymbals,
praise him with resounding cymbals.
Let everything that has breath praise the LORD.
Praise the LORD.*

PSALM 150

AS YOU PRAISE GOD TODAY

- Think of three ways God has blessed you, and praise him for them.
- Think about who he is and praise God for all of his many wonderful attributes.

SOURCES

Baloche, Paul. *Praise Adonai.* Mobile, AL: Integrity's Hosanna Music, 1999.

Boa, Kenneth. *Face to Face: Praying the Scriptures for Spiritual Growth.* Grand Rapids, MI: Zondervan, 1997.

Boa, Kenneth. *The Two-Year Daily Reading and Prayer Bible.* Grand Rapids, MI: Zondervan, 1997.

Bosworth, Fred Francis. *Christ the Healer.* Grand Rapids, MI: Baker Book House, 1973.

Brownlow, Leroy. *A Psalm in My Heart.* Fort Worth, TX: Brownlow Publishing Company, 1989.

Chambers, Oswald, Reimann, James, ed. *My Utmost for His Highest,* updated edition. Grand Rapids, MI: Discovery House Publishers, 1995.

Christian Growth Study Bible. Grand Rapids, MI: Zondervan, 1997.

Classics Devotional Bible. Grand Rapids, MI: Zondervan, 1996.

Cowman, L.B. Reimann, James, ed. *Streams in the Desert,* updated edition. Grand Rapids, MI: Zondervan, 1997.

Cowman, Mrs. Charles E. *Streams in the Desert 1.* Cowman Publications, Inc. 1965.

Draper, Edythe. *Draper's Book of Quotations for the Christian World.* Wheaton, IL: Tyndale House.

Gaither, Gloria. *Because He Lives.* Grand Rapids, MI: Zondervan, 1997.

Gire, Ken. *Intense Moments with the Savior.* Grand Rapids, MI: Zondervan, 1994.

Hudson, Robert R. and Townsend-Hudson, Shelley. *Companions for the Soul.* Grand Rapids, MI: Zondervan , 1995.

Hupp, Sarah M. *Daily Prayer From the New International Version.* Grand Rapids, MI: Zondervan, 2001.

Keller, Phillip. *A Shepherd Looks at Psalm 23.* Grand Rapids, MI: Zondervan, 1981.

Kruidenier, William. *The Life Promises Bible.* Grand Rapids, MI: Zondervan, 2001.

Manser, Martin H. *The Westminster Collection of Christian Quotations.* Louisville, KY: Westminster John Knox Press, 2001.

McLaren, Brian D. *Finding Faith.* Grand Rapids, MI: Zondervan, 1999.

NIV Couples Devotional Bible. Grand Rapids, MI: Zondervan, 1994.

NIV Mom's Devotional Bible. Grand Rapids, MI: Zondervan, 1996.

NIV Worship Bible. Grand Rapids, MI: Zondervan, 2000.

Ortberg, John. *The Life You've Always Wanted.* Grand Rapids, MI: Zondervan, 1997

Reflecting God Study Bible. Grand Rapids, MI: Zondervan, 2000

Ryken, Leland, James C. Wilhoit, Tremper Longman, III, *Dictionary of Biblical Imagery.* Downers Grove, IL: InterVarsity Press, 1998.

Smith, Huston. *Beyond the Post-Modern Mind.* Quest Books, 1989.

Smith, Martin. *Shout to the North*. Music UK/Adminis-
tered in North America by EMI Christian, 1995.

Spangler, Ann and Jean E Syswerda. *Women of the Bible*.
Grand Rapids, MI: Zondervan, 1999.

Stanley, Charles. *A Touch of His Love*. Grand Rapids, MI:
Zondervan, 1994. *A Touch of His Freedom*. Grand
Rapids, MI: Zondervan, 1991. *A Touch of His Peace*.
Grand Rapids, MI: Zondervan, 1993. *A Touch of His
Wisdom*. Grand Rapids, MI: Zondervan, 1992.

Strong, John. *Strong's Exhaustive Concordance*. Grand
Rapids, MI: Baker Book House.

Troccoli, Kathy. *My Life Is in Your Hands*. Grand
Rapids, MI: Zondervan, 1997.

Wangerin Jr., Walter. *Whole Prayer*. Grand Rapids, MI:
Zondervan, 1998.

Water, Mark. *The New Encyclopedia of Christian Quotations*. Grand Rapids, MI: Baker Books, 2000.